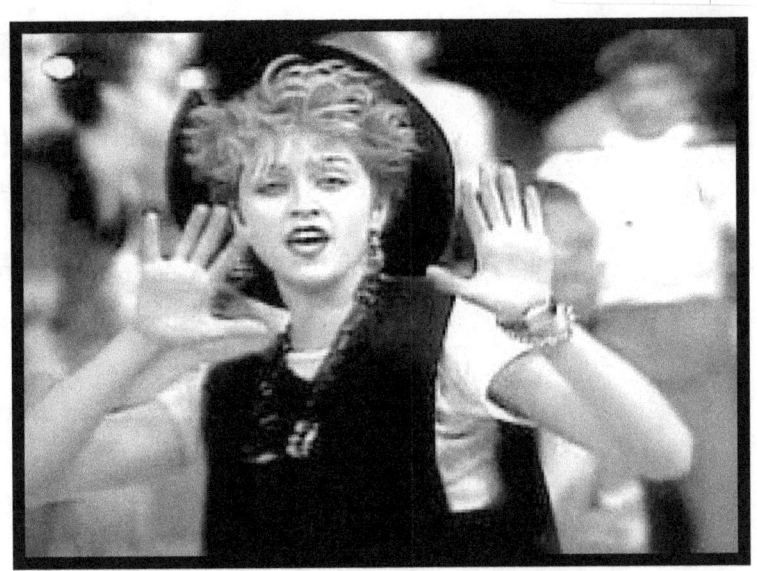

MADONNA

IN THE EIGHTIES

Chris Wade

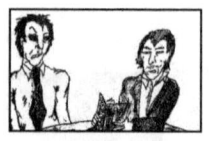

Madonna in the Eighties
by Chris Wade

Wisdom Twins Books, 2018
wisdomtwinsbooks.weebly.com

This edition released in 2018

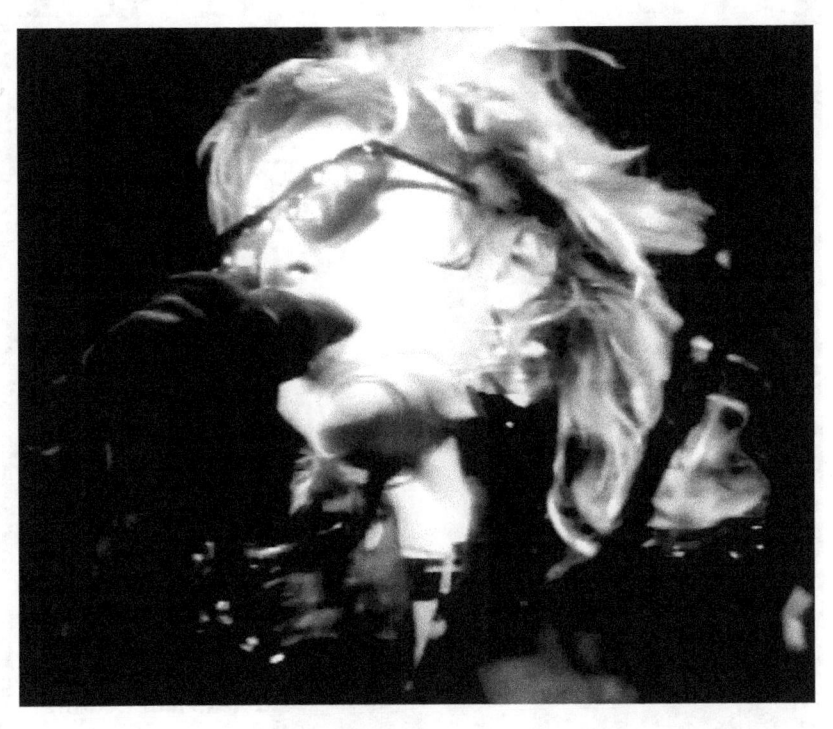

MADONNA

IN THE EIGHTIES

MADONNA

WHO'S THAT GIRL WORLD TOUR 1987

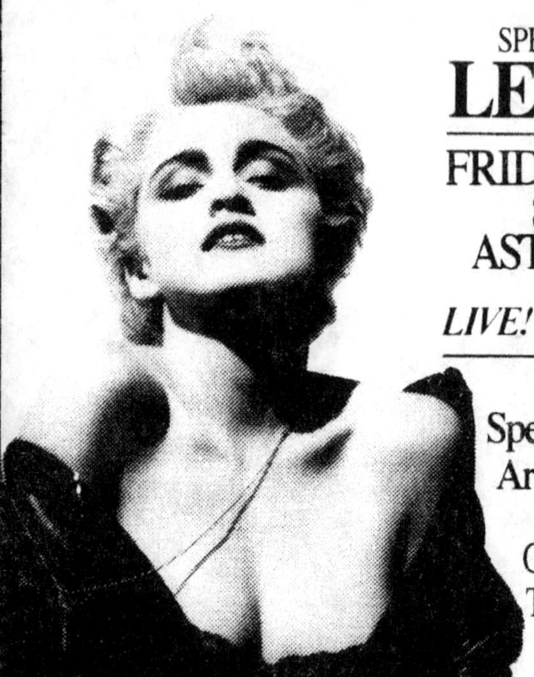

SPECIAL GUEST

LEVEL 42

FRIDAY, JULY 24
8:00PM
ASTRODOME

LIVE! IN CONCERT!

Special State of The Art Sound System

Giant Video Screen
Theatrical Seating!!

TONIGHT!

Buy Early! Seating Limited due to special Theatrical Staging.

TICKETS AVAILABLE AT TICKETRON OUTLETS INCLUDING FOLEY'S, FIESTA FOOD MARTS, ASTRODOME BOX OFFICE AND ALL OTHER TICKETRON LOCATIONS

CHARGE BY PHONE **(713) 526-1709**

FOR MORE INFORMATION: 799-9555

PRODUCED BY PACE CONCERTS

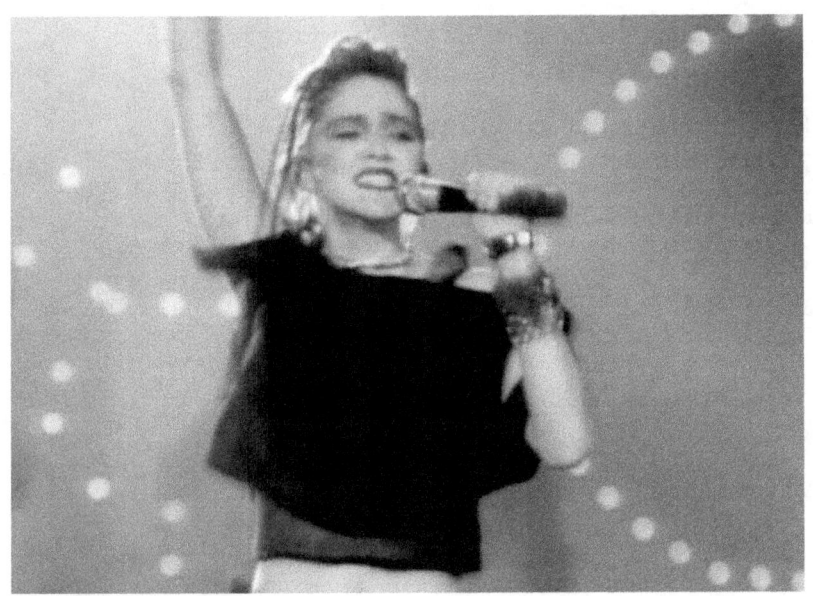

CONTENTS

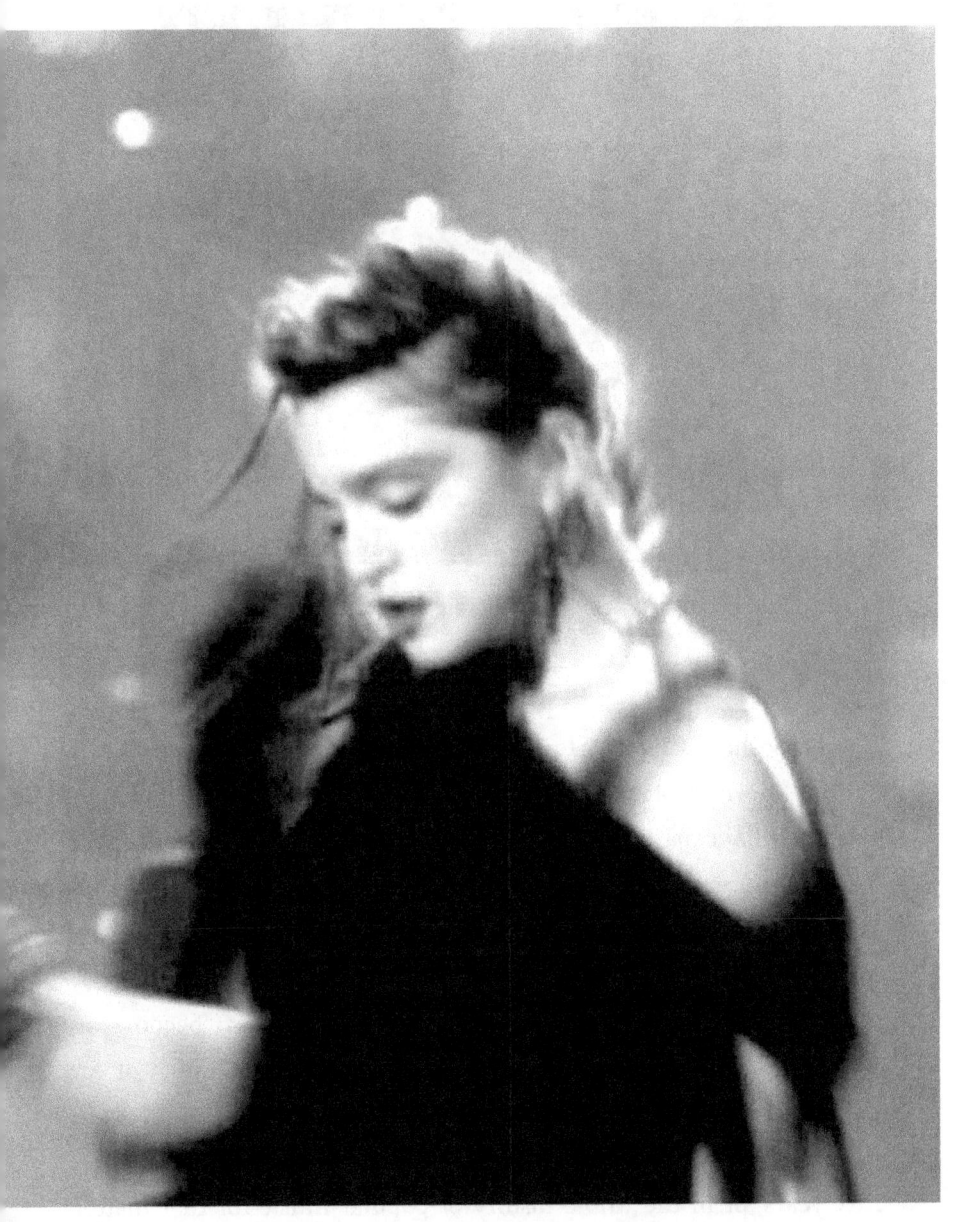

Madonna performing Holiday on TV.

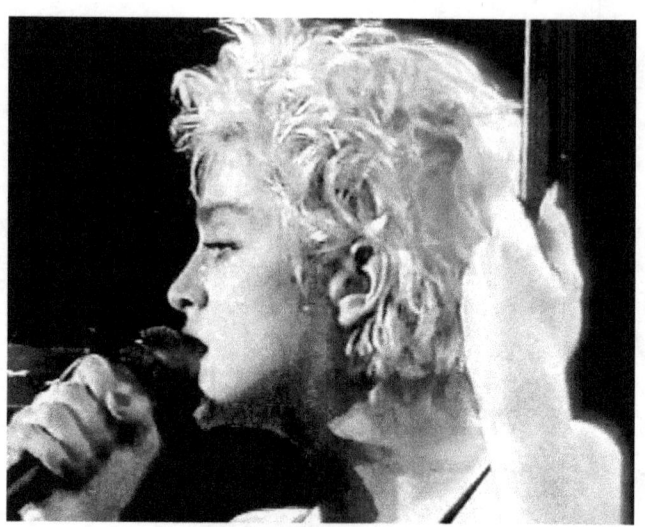

INTRODUCTION

AN ICON FOR THE EIGHTIES

The belly shot of Lucky Star; the rolling about on the boat in Like A Virgin; the short blonde hair cut and 'Italians Do It Better T Shirt' fin the video for Papa Don't Preach; the beach frolicking of Cherish; the Marilyn inspired glamour of Material Girl; the hippy look of Like A Prayer... All this and I'm not even into the 1990s yet. I'm talking about, of course, the iconography of Madonna in the 1980s.

The image and visual identity of Madonna has become as important as her music, if not more so in the eyes of much of the public. That said, Madonna's discography does contain some of the most memorable, widely played and brilliant songs made in the last fifty years, or in the whole history of popular music for that matter. But having emerged in the boom of MTV and the music video,

Madonna knew all too well that when combining a solid tune with a memorable video, the commercial feedback would be out of this world, or potentially at least. Having the birth name Madonna helped (now that's a name and a statement at the same time), and proved she was halfway there in getting people's attentions before they even met her. What is more iconic than the figure of the Madonna herself? Perhaps Madonna Ciccone was born (in Detroit, in 1958 as it happens) knowing she was to be put on a pedestal and looked upon as a notable figure. This adoration took years of grafting to earn though, and the Queen slaved for her crown. Calling her a figure of worship doesn't seem that over the top either, especially when you consider that world wide loyal following she has. From the word go, she knew how an image, a style and a presence could command not only a room, but a wider public, a nation, a whole species for that matter. From her first album, she put herself firmly into the centre of pop culture, firstly through her music (those early catchy hits), and then with that unforgettable, unshakeable, firm iconography.

The almost clichéd idea of Madonna remains the one of the mid 80s, the standard adopted hen party outfit, the Desperately Seeking Susan get up with the lacy clothes, wild hair and punk inspired street quality. For many it's the quintessential Madonna image, but it was of course only the very beginning. UK fans first caught her on the Tube and Top of the Pops in 83 and 84, and in no time at all copycat Madonnas were everywhere. If they weren't singing her songs, they were at least looking like her and that mixed rag tag image that came from the New York dance scene. Madonna absorbed it and gave it to the world as a gift, in return for eternal fame and success.

Madonna's early image was punk inspired, but it was also lifted from elements of what was going on at the time. However catchy her early disco pop songs were, it was the very image of Madonna that caught people's attention the most. After all, she had never wanted to be a singer per se, primarily wishing to dance and act. Music was a way, in effect, to get people to look and pay attention to her. And it worked. Madonna's dark make up, torn clothes, mix of jewellery and accessories imbedded her into the world's minds. She hadn't quite mastered her vocals yet (this is 1983-4 we are talking about), so she made up for it in other ways; her humour, her attitude, her bounciness, sex appeal and clothes. She was a pop star in everyway, and a real personality. Madonna the alley cat, street wise urchin was also something of an image in itself, though an image formed through a life style. She came to New York with 50 dollars and ate out of bins before making the big time and becoming the female icon of the 1980s.

"It's fashionable to slum," Madonna told Interview Magazine in 1984 about her transition from scene girl to pop megastar. "To live with five people in an apartment and to wear the same outfit every day, to never comb your hair and to live on jellybeans - no pun intended. You know, half the people I hung out with from the downtown area have totally snubbed me. They think that I'm selling out and stuff. If I go back to clubs they won't talk to me. Nasty little digs like, 'Little Madonna, now she's a big star and she can't talk to us.' That's why I don't feel a real unity with all those people, because half of them have totally ousted me anyway. They say like, Oh, she never really hung out anyway, she's not really downtown."

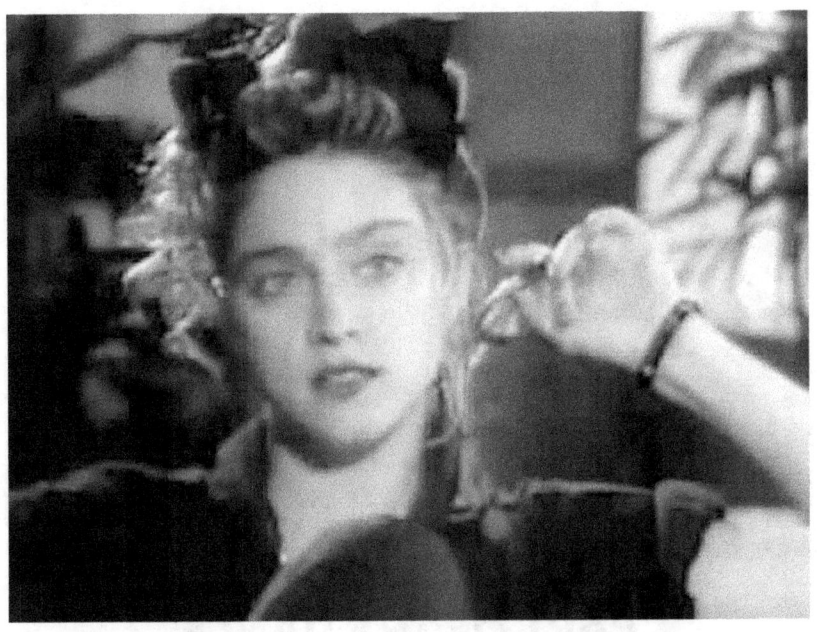

The ragged street punk was just the first Madonna persona. Whether Madonna truly lived any of her 80s identities is anyone's guess, but she did "become" each one, if only before the public, in concert, in her movies, on her albums and in her videos. By taking on a new image and look what seemed like every week, Madonna became the everywoman of the 1980s; the punk, the pop princess, the virgin, the material girl, the whore, the film star, the pin up, the feminist, the anti feminist, the new age being of self awareness, the fun loving party girl. She was all this and more, all in the one decade she helped to shape and carve into eternity. This book features various essays on the work she created and unleashed in that decade, starting with her music videos, her albums, films and concert tours. It's a remarkable body of work, one which grows in influence and importance as the years go by.

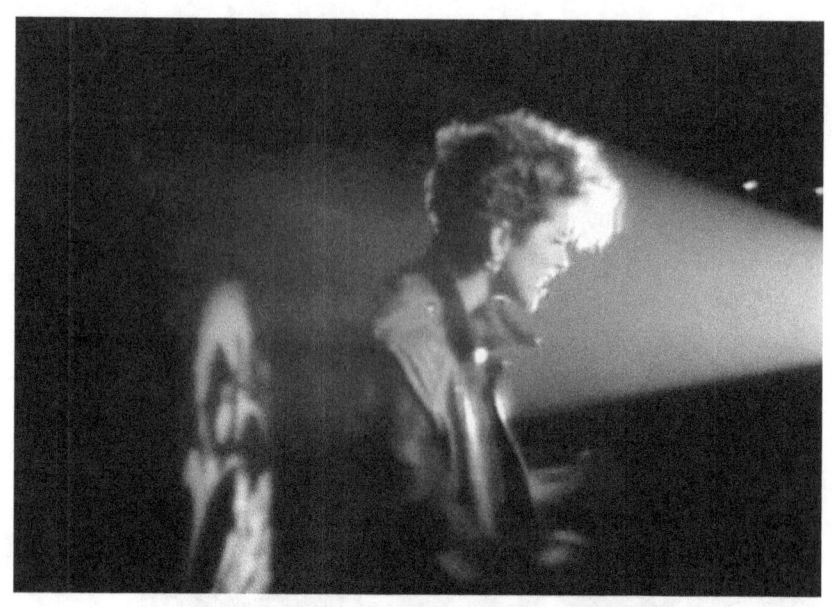

PART OF THE DANCE
SEXUAL POLITICS AND
MADONNA'S EARLY VIDEOS

As is so often said, Madonna was made by MTV is the general theory; but you could also safely say the reverse was true too, that Madonna in turn made MTV. In fact, the realm of the music video was just another area of 80s culture which Madonna dominated. She led fashion trends to the point that every young girl wanted to look and dress like her; she influenced and led the charts with classic single after classic single; she led the way in terms of pop albums too, shifting multi millions of records and pushing the boundaries of popular music at the same time. These were just some of the areas where she reigned supreme, but she was not without criticism of course. While some saw her as an icon for feminism, others thought she actually brought feminism back thirty years - which is, of course, nonsense. She was a powerful woman, the new female for the 1980s - ambitious, sexy, daring and fearless.

One area which she excelled in, without question, was in the music video, and what better place is there to start in terms of Madonna's progression and take over as the leading video artist of our age, than the very beginning? Judging by her debut music video, the ultra low budget promo for her first single, Everybody, no one could have truly believed that Madonna would become the most important, popular, revolutionary and innovative music star of the MTV generation. The single, put out in 1982 ahead of her first album (which emerged the year after), was a dance floor hit in New York, but seeing as she wasn't (yet) a touring artist, a promo video was deemed necessary to send out in order to spread the word. If Madonna couldn't play to the people in the flesh, then her video would. "If I didn't have a video, I don't think all the kids in the Midwest would know about me," she later said. "It takes the place of touring. Everybody sees them everywhere. That really has a lot to do with the success of my album."

Ed Steinberg, who ran the Rock America Company, was given a thousand dollar budget to shoot the promo, a sum that seems unbelievable today, given the huge budgets of her later videos. The song, of course, is what really did the selling here; Everybody is a bouncy, bright and bubbly pop classic, with a sexy Madonna vocal and some uplifting synths, noises and beats. The video, with a distinct no frills approach, is actually very well shot. Featuring a host of her friends as extras (her friend Debi Mazar did the make up), Madonna

13

sings and dances on a stage, in her vintage style, as the disco lights whirl and twirl, the silhouetted revellers let loose to the music. With her hair punked up and her constantly-moving body clad in one of the least showy outfits of her music video career, it's understandable why some would overlook this slightly underwhelming piece. Personally, though, I find its low-key feel refreshing, and I like the fact that the focus is on Madonna's charisma alone and, most importantly in my view, the song itself. For a new artist, such a video was to be expected. But if anything, the lack of visual distractions and artistic goals for the video being a stand alone film probably did Madonna a world of good. After all, she is the central focal point here, and all eyes are on her.

What is clear from this video though, and even at this extremely early stage in both her recording career and her career as a primal, important video artist, is that she commands the camera. She is using her sexuality with control, and though only 25 here, she seems like a woman set on a path she has laid out for herself, a journey to a destiny of her own making. You can also see the excitement, the determination to make heads turn, to grab the attention of everyone watching. She is a woman who had done so much already, slaved and worked away as a backing dancer, a drummer, a model... you name it, she had done it. And here it was, her first chance at the big time. How much the video did for Madonna's single becoming a hit cannot be fully defined, at least not as much as it can be for her future videos. Unfortunately, it seems to have drifted into obscurity (as much as anything Madonna related can); it wasn't put on to Madonna's double DVD video collection Celebration, nor did it feature on the landmark

60 minute video, The Immaculate Collection, which was released in 1990.

I spoke to Ed Steinberg all about the video. "I had been part of the 'crew' surrounding Madonna - Mark Kamims, Michael Rosenblatt etc.," Ed told me in 2017. "Seymour Stein (music entrepreneur) had asked me to shoot one of Madonna's shows at Howie's No Entendes performances at Danceteria. But I felt a simple music video would be more fun and useful. So I was allowed to use Paradise Garage for a day. Madonna was a 'featured' extra in a video I directed for a New York based funk group, Konk. My formal introduction was with Michael Rosenblatt inviting me to dinner with Madonna at a fancy seafood restaurant in Manhattan. But I had seen her around and was friendly with her for a while. She was always 'on the scene' like the rest of us. Intense clubbing and attending multiple band performances each night."

On the subject of the shoot itself, Ed told me it took "the better part of a (long) day. It was scheduled to start at 8 a.m. The crew set up at 8 but Madonna's choice of makeup person, Debbie Mazar, showed up about 90 minutes late. But it worked out OK as one of M's dancers was late and it turned out never showed up. The choreography was purely Madonna's. I just had to re-block it as one of the dancers never showed and we needed to compensate for the clubs' stage. It was an extremely low budget so we needed to make due with what we had. Baggs and Erik were easy to work with. Good dancers and knew Madonna's choreography. "

As for the video now, looking back on his early work, Ed said,"well, for a $1,000 budget it's good... very good. It gets Madonna's song across and shows her in a very good light. Would I have liked more money to do more? Naturally. I actually did spend $4,500 on the shoot. I actually paid all of the crew! For me, Everybody was the link between '70's Disco and '80's New Wave; or as we called it then, DOR - Dance Oriented Music. It was both pop and dance. Good and clearly successful combination of music styles culminating with a familiar song you could dance to and hum. Even as a novice singer/performer, I realized she was something else. Despite needing to reblock the set and perform for one camera maybe 40 times or more she maintained her cool and was a pleasure to work with. Rumours persisted about Madonna's being very difficult to work with. But I never found that in this video or the many of her remix videos we later created for her many songs."

For many (but only because fewer people have seen Everybody), the first true Madonna promo video was her second, the raw but slightly more elaborate and polished Burning Up. The song is Madonna at her early best; poppy and punchy, with a catchy chorus, a charismatic performance and some very exciting music. The video, directed by Steve Barron, is pure pop art camp, images of cool cars and boats, flashing eyes in statues, a directorial flair which instantly elevates the video up a level from the plain and simply restricted Everybody. Here, out of the confines of the darkly lit disco hall, Madonna has already become a star. Madonna, in her white outfit, looks every bit an icon, as she rolls and cavorts in the middle of a suburban street at night, owning the road. The black and white close ups are equally brilliant, with Madonna's face bursting with wild electricity. When she's wearing the classic chain from the LP cover, she bounces around like a child. In the end though, it's her passion that strikes the most, both the song and the video working together

16

to establish Madonna as a sexual being to be taken seriously. This is not light, inconsequential fluff to be sung by anyone with a half-decent voice and a pretty face, and she is no passive pop princess to be merely ogled; she is a presence to take notice of, to idolise, a figure to adorn your bedroom wall. This is it, the moment she becomes Madonna. Importantly, while Madonna waits for her man in his topless sports car to arrive, in the end it is *she* who drives away in the car. Here, in a tidy little image at the very end of the video, she is telling the world who is the boss, who is dominant and who is going to be in charge of the rest of her life and career - and that is, of course, herself.

Burning Up was not a big hit upon its release, but its video has become an important landmark moment in terms of Madonna's visual and musical development. She has since covered it live, most recently - rather wonderfully I might add - on her Rebel Heart tour. The version on her latest live DVD (titled simply Rebel Heart Tour) has Madonna holding an electric guitar, chugging away powerfully at the strings, smacking out power chords like some rock goddess with high heels and long legs (even though she's diminutive, she often looks towering). She proves the song is still as commanding as ever, a theme for self-empowerment, for the female taking control of her own life and love, not just waiting for the man to arrive.

Lucky Star is where it all truly began though, her first Top 5 hit in the US, released two months after her debut album had hit the shelves. Seeing the video now really takes you back to 1983, and just how impactful and fresh Madonna was at the time. The video, directed by Arthur Pierson, begins with a black and white close up of the pop princess herself, removing her sunglasses and staring into the camera. The reveal of her eyes turns the video to colour, though the simplicity of the video itself doesn't really need much colour to pack its meaty punch. Set to a white background and done up in her classic cut-up punk style (fishnet top, clear gloves, messy hair held in by a bow, subtle make up, baggy shorts), Madonna only needs herself and two dancers to hold the visual attention for 4 minutes. There are no effects, no extras, no arty scenarios or detours - just Madonna, the (lucky) star of 83 shining brightly. She brings the song to life, its simplicity matching the bareness of the background and the directness of Madonna's body movements. It is telling that such a plain and simple video keeps you hooked, and also a credit not only to Madonna's charisma, but also the song itself, which is pure pop gold, sounding as vital and urgent as ever before, even 35 years later. Madonna closes the video by putting her glasses back on, and bringing our world back to black and white, after brightening and colouring it up so wonderfully for those breezy four minutes.

Borderline, released as a single in 1984 but also a part of the debut LP, is the first Madonna video to have more than one layer to it, even though Burning Up did have the image of the young man in the car racing to retrieve his lusty love. Here though, Madonna is seen interacting with others, while still managing to keep hold of 95 percent of the viewer's attention. It was also her first collaboration with Mary Lambert, with whom she would make some of the most important videos of the era.

Borderline starts with a slowed down sequence of Madonna dancing with some street kids in a gritty urban area. They are in rapture, joyously setting themselves free through dance. Madonna, in cut off denim jacket and red headband, sticks out from the others though. She catches the eye of a photographer in a smooth suit, who hands her a card. As he photographs her, Madonna sings to the camera in black and white, her hair wild, her expression commanding our attention. She is also seen in various contrived positions as the photographer snaps away. In between these arranged black and white shots, where Madonna keeps the song going while acting for the camera, she is driven around by another man, this one younger, more like the urbanites at the start of the video. Still, in the more "glamorous" segments, she kisses her photographer, the man who seems to have plucked her from obscurity and promised some kind of fame, but she seems more at home and confident on the streets, blowing kisses to the boy, laughing on the corners with her friends. She reveals a sensitivity too, clearly troubled by how her boyfriend is hurt by her relationship with the photographer, and perhaps a little jealous of the attention she is getting, especially when he picks up a magazine on a newsstand with her on the cover. Destiny has its way in the end though, and when Madonna spray paints the lavish photography set (you can take the girl out of the street, but you can't take the street out of the girl), he snaps at her, is enraged and tells her to get out. Where does she go? Back to the street, where she feels a part of something, and back into the arms of her true love.

These days, one could look at the Borderline video and see the irony of it. After all, here is this street savvy punk, taken in by the lure of fame and money, temporarily abandoning her roots and all

19

she has left behind until she realises success, money and the so called glitz of celebrity are not what they seem. Madonna explored this theme more thoroughly in the late 90s and beyond, when she had actually personally lived through the disappointments of fame, and the trappings of having every camera lens in the world ready to snap away at you when you least expect it. Here though, Madonna the bright eyed 25 year old (she looks younger in this video to be fair) has all this ahead of her. The bigger irony is in the fact that the Madonna character in the video actually gives up on the idea of fame (or seems to at least) and goes back to the streets. In reality, Madonna outgrew the underground New York club scene and many of her old friends, and became the most famous woman on the planet. She certainly crossed a Borderline all of her own.

Still, as entertainment, the video was a stepping stone towards her more story orientated promos, and it also marked a point when we saw the effects Madonna had on men, more directly so. The photographer turns to mush and panders pathetically, until he realises he cannot contain her of course. By portraying the spunky boy toy she was off camera - pretty but tough, feminine but headstrong - Madonna established her powerful stance early on, and subtly, within the confines of a music promo video.

Borderline was her first major chart hit, and no doubt the video did it some good. Lambert's direction is classy and on the money, every shot bringing out the vitality and character of Madonna's face. They tend to say she was never a natural beauty, but she looks extraordinary in the Borderline video, ands seemingly with very little care given to her make up and outfits. This was Madonna circa 83/84, presented as was - and the world loved it.

"When I screened Borderline for Madonna's manager, Freddy DeMann," Lambert later said, "he was hysterical that I had combined black-and-white footage with colour footage. Nobody had done that before. He made me screen it for all the secretaries in the office and see how they reacted, because he felt I had crossed a line that shouldn't be crossed."

Borderline may have pushed boundaries, but Like A Virgin, for me, is where it all changes, and from here on after every Madonna video is a film with itself, as vital a creation as the song it's accompanying, and just as important as a separate piece of art. That's not to say that her previous videos weren't good, because they clearly were, and still are. However, for me, this is the point where Madonna really brings her acting talent to the videos, her dedication and control (her status as a "performance artist" truly starts here I believe) and takes on so many roles and characters that it becomes dizzying when trying to take them all in together in one go. It is a gallery of faces, creations, rather like Robert De Niro in his prime immersing himself in his roles. Comparing her to the Greatest American Actor of our time seems over the top, but watch those classics videos again and you will see that Madonna seems to live and breathe these parts.

That said, I do not think the Like A Virgin video is better than Borderline. If anything, it's less unified, getting by more on Madonna's cavorting than any flow or story line. Still, it's down to Madonna's look, her magnetism, and Lambert's loose style, lacking in fussiness here, which make the video a classic.

"For Like a Virgin I said 'Lets do it in Venice!' The idea of Madonna singing in a gondola was the most outrageous thing I could think of," Lambert said later. "And Madonna dug it, because she has the whole

21

thing with the Catholic Church and her Italian heritage. It turned into a huge party."

The video portrays Madonna as both the virgin in white and the sexual being in black, restlessly wriggling on the gondola one minute, but trying to elude the loose lion the next, all in pure white, who is on the prowl through the winding streets and towering pillars. If the lion represents the male, and the impending reality of the sensual world (however wildly erotic or compromised it might be), the flow of the water upon which Madonna is in control of herself and her sexuality, stands as self belief, being comfortable in ones' own skin and behind the steering wheel. Provocative in more of an arty, abstract manner than anything literal, the video triggers thoughts of sexual morals, the jungle that is love and the animalistic nature of seeking a mate. It is all this and more, both consciously and perhaps subconsciously, but importantly it did what the record label (Warners) wanted it to do - sell Madonna to the world as a hot new talent. It also proved that though Madonna was in the pop game, she could underline her more conventional work with thought provoking views on more adult, controversial themes.

It wouldn't be the last time Madonna would work with one of the larger cat family (observe the tiger in her 1987 film, Who's That Girl?), but she enjoyed her interactions with the lion while making the Like A Virgin video.

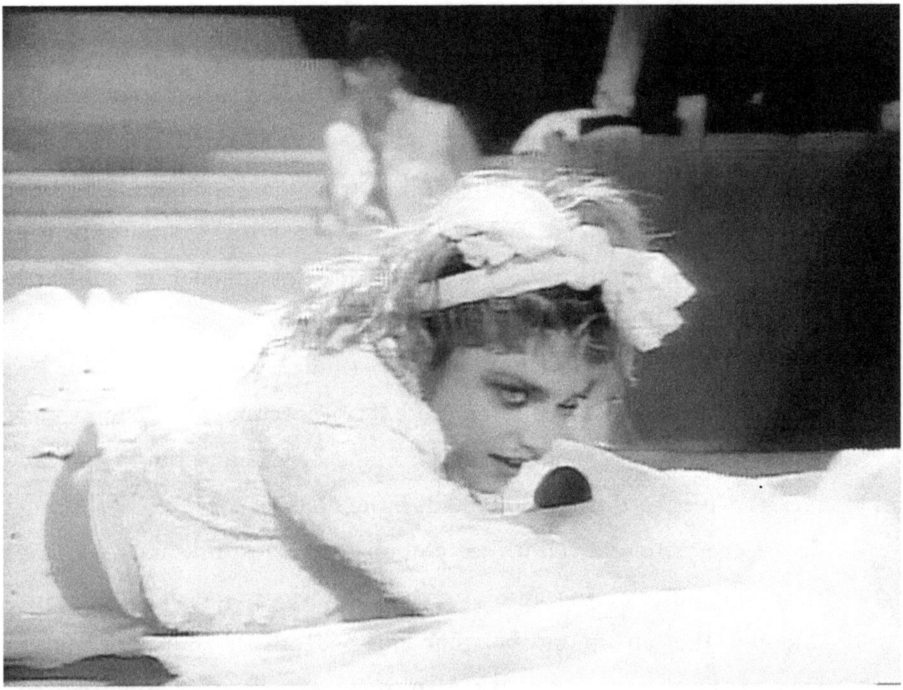

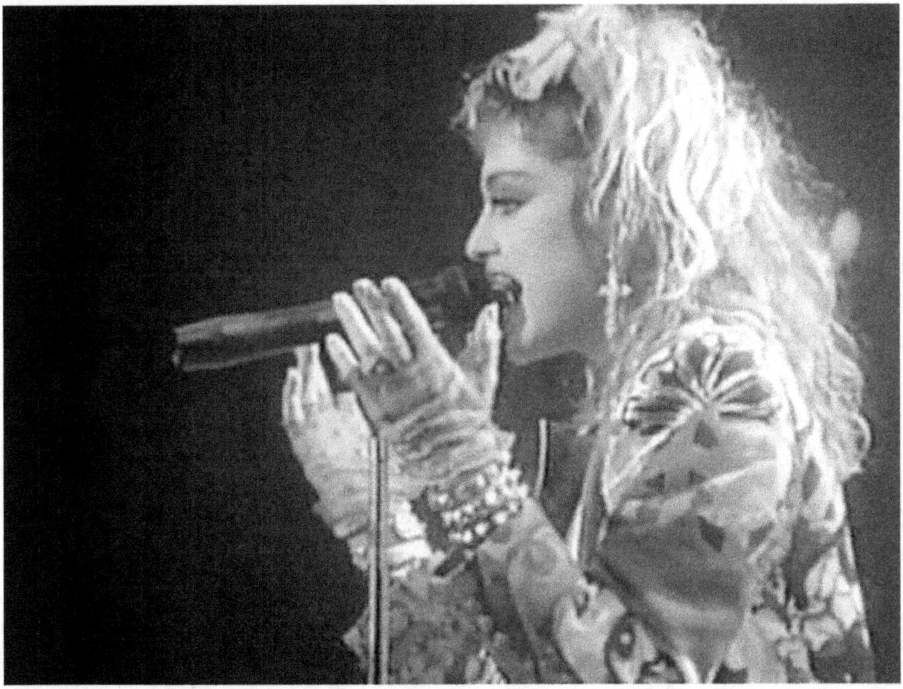

"The lion didn't do anything he was supposed to do," she said, "and I ended up leaning against this pillar with his head in my crotch... I thought he was going to take a bite out of me so I lifted the veil I was wearing and had a stare-down with him and he opened his mouth and let out this huge roar. I got so frightened my heart fell in my shoe. When he finally walked away, the director yelled 'Cut' and I had to take a long breather. But I could really relate to the lion. I feel like in a past life I was a lion or a cat or something."

Though Madonna has often said it is not one of her personal favourite songs, it was the one that made her a household name all over the globe; the video, whether she liked it or not, was being played everywhere. Even if the symbolism was lost on many viewers, it was an entertaining mini movie, on the surface an advert for Madonna the pin up and pop star, but beneath the shiny exterior a deep meditation on sexuality. Venice, to Madonna, "symbolized so many things, like virginity. And I'm Madonna, and I'm Italian." Clearly, there was no better place than Venice for the cross loving provocateur to turn sexuality on its head. Even if the cavorting Madonna was a twist on the public's perception of her, it was the Madonna the world would be seeing at face value, regardless of the metaphorical meaning.

Even from the five videos covered in this piece, Madonna had firmly set her own rule book, by which she and many other copyists would then follow. These days, music videos are often more important than the song itself as a product (they are basically selling the video, not the single), but it's hard to imagine how fresh this must have been back in the day. I was not born, but that doesn't mean I cannot understand how astonishing Madonna must have seemed with her advanced views on sexuality and the sureness with which she conducted herself. There had been no one like her before. Sure, women had been empowered in the music industry, but Madonna changed it all. She looks, to put it simply, totally in control, not only of herself, but her music, her image, her audience, and perhaps most of all, her sexual power.

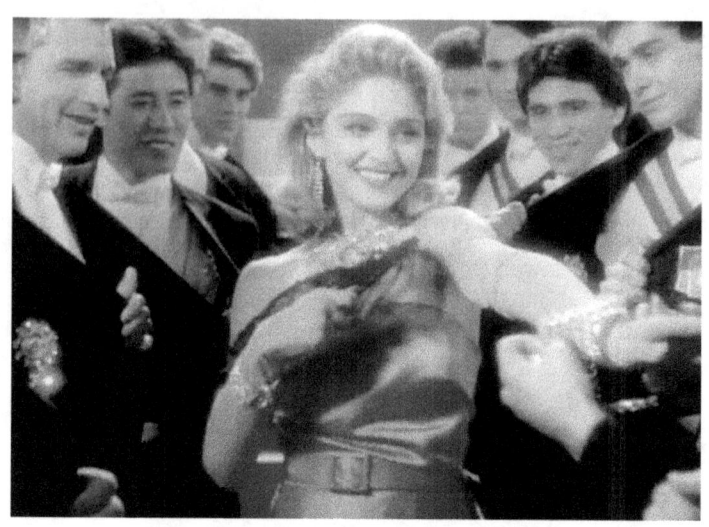

THE ICON IS BORN
HOW MADONNA TOOK OVER MTV

Madonna may have used MTV as a selling tool to package herself and her music to the world, but if those songs hadn't been so good (and so damned catchy) then after a couple of videos the bubble would have burst, the Madonna hype would have died down and everyone would have gone on to something else. But Madonna was at the top of her game when it came to ideas, to twisting the world's perception of the female and her sexuality, selling herself as a powerful woman for a new age. The music was co -written and played by expert session men, but the overall theme belonged to Madonna. With her songs and videos, she was essentially holding up a mirror to society; to the greedy suits chasing the dollar, to the sexist male wolf whistling the passing women.

At the start of 1985, bang centre in the middle of the decade of yuppies, excess and hard cash, Madonna emerged with one of the punchiest, funniest and most effective song-video combos in music history. The song was Material Girl, a track culled from her second album, Like A Virgin. It was a playful, poppy jab at the 'greed is good' ethics of the eighties, where the female narrator spends the whole song courting rich men, and in the end turns the table on them all and pronounces herself the one with the money and the upper hand. We are all living in a material world is what she was saying; but of course, with the world not always being attuned to the definition of irony, it was taken as a blatant statement. "I am Madonna and I like material things" is how most people saw it. Of course, the whole thing was social satire.

The video was directed by Mary Lambert (her third Madonna video on the trot) and featured the new princess of pop as a star being perused by a rich film producer, played by Keith Carradine. Most of the action comes in the film within the film, where the producer and a fellow film industry figure (played by David Wuhl) watch Madonna on a screen, done up as Marilyn Monroe in her famous pink outfit for the step dance number in Diamonds Are A Girl's Best Friend. Madonna looks much younger, softer in the face and cheekier than Monroe, but she channels her inner film goddess perfectly. Some might say that this represents the peak of her acting career, but I have to disagree. Though her performance is sublime in this brief snapshot, it is all too brief to be fully fleshed out. Indeed, I could have easily watched a whole movie done in this fashion, the action dipping in and out of reality; Madonna the star on the big screen, larger than life, and Madonna the woman off screen as seen in the

27

eyes of the male. But a snapshot it is, and Madonna is superb at being the object of every man's desire, rich or poor, everyday Joe or powerful film producer. As the suited chaps gawp and hang on her every movement on the stairs, it's all so convincing that you wonder how much acting had to be done by the guys.

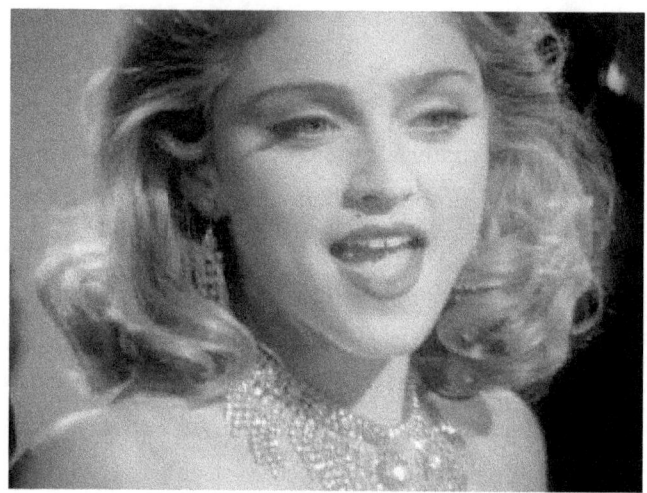

A still from the Material Girl video.

Though only on her second album at this point, Madonna was now a household name, a fully formed celebrity. The world had its idea of Madonna, her fans had theirs, as did the media, and to the media she was a man eating sex bomb who had done whatever she had to do to get to the top of the music business. They chose to ignore the years of grafting and hard work, of poverty, stealing food from bins and doing odd jobs to make ends meet while pursuing her dream. Now, only a few singles and videos into her career, Madonna was there as a person for everyone to figure out, define and judge, whether they knew her personally or not. She had sold herself as a sexy woman in her promo videos, but had she known just how much she would be objectified by every man out there I wonder if she would have pushed so hard to - as she put it herself on American Bandstand - rule the world.

For Madonna, Marilyn Monroe was "it", the most famous woman that had ever lived (until Madonna came along, that is), and she related to her in many ways; mostly in her sexuality, how she had become sexualised so much that her figure and appearance overshadowed the person she had become. Madonna knew she was in danger of becoming this way too, so she lampooned the whole idea of the sex symbol before the camera. More importantly, though, she related to Monroe's vulnerability, the tenderness behind the iconic images and the sexy poster girl poses. Still, Madonna knew she would not be a victim of fame and the microscopic lens it invites, but an empowered feminine role model, the likes of which the world had never seen before. To say she is still active thirty odd years later, still pissing off and delighting people in equal measure (no one divides people quite like Madonna) proves that she fulfilled her goal. it also proves how strong she was and still is.

"Well, my favourite scene in all of Monroe's movies is when she does that dance sequence for Diamonds Are a Girl's Best Friend," Madonna told New York Daily News. "And when it came time to do the video for the song I said, I can just redo that whole scene and it will be perfect. Marilyn was made into something not human in a way, and I can relate to that. Her sexuality was something everyone was obsessed with and that I can relate to. And there were certain

29

things about her vulnerability that I'm curious about and attracted to..."

"I have always been extremely interested in Marilyn Monroe," Lambert herself told Rolling Stone, "her life and persona. Madonna and I shared that fascination. I watched the dance sequence from Gentlemen Prefer Blondes about a million times with Kenny Ortega (choreographer), who brilliantly reinterpreted it for the film. Material Girl was my first collaboration with costume designer Marlene Stewart, who brilliantly reinterpreted the dress. If you have a very specific vision in mind, work with talented people, that's my advice."

Material Girl is a prime example where the video not only perfectly accompanies the song, but improves upon it, becoming an essential counterpart in the process. The message in the video is different to what the song itself delivers. The producer only manages to woo Madonna when he disguises as a poor man and offers her heartfelt warmth, cheap plastic flowers, not material objects, which she clearly does not need. Then, as if to whisk her away from the shallow world of show business, he drives her off, not in a sports car or a chauffeur driven limo, but a dirty old truck, in which they passionately kiss at the video's end. The song however, has a more ironic twist; Madonna has saved up her money and now all the guys are after her. But it's the message in the video which makes more sense as a fully realised message, and mirrors Madonna's own views the closest. Less ironic, more real.

If Material Girl isn't her most iconic video, then it is certainly right up there. It created a new iconography for Madonna, which ironically wasn't really her own. Though she put a slant on the Monroe man eater image, she had updated it, made it more conscious by presenting it to the viewer as a film within a film, with tongue firmly in cheek. When Taylor Swift performed her single Shake It Off at the 2014 MTV Video Music Awards, she wasn't really paying tribute to Monroe; no, her homage was to Madonna. For this new generation (and indeed the two or so before it, in Madonna's artistic lifetime as a public cultural icon), it is *her* who is the reference point, not Monroe and the likes; at least not to the degree Madonna has become the figure of her time.

Some have criticised the way Madonna pays homage to something and brings it into her work, thus claiming it her own, but influence is what all true great art is about, and I find what others have called her "cultural vampirism" is actually one of her greatest qualities. She can present an image (or a sound of course), turn it on its head and make it into something new. She's been doing it for over thirty years now.

Material Girl then, I feel, is the first instance where we see Madonna really in control of herself and everyone around her. If the earlier videos had suggested she might be the new female being for the 1980s, vulnerable and powerful at the same time, then Material Girl stamped this theory firmly on to the surface. Ironic or not, Madonna established herself as the woman all men wanted - and in visual terms, especially for an MTV audience, this was taken literally, rather than in the spirit of the good camp humour it was intended. Besides, this is not merely some one dimensional portrayal of Madonna as shallow power-woman at the centre of every male's attention, desiring material objects like some hungry commercialised beast. We must remember, the Monroe homage sequence is a contrived scene within the music video itself, a part her character is playing up on the big screen. The "real" Madonna in the video is humbled and won over by cheap flowers and a mucky old truck. If this didn't make the message of the video obvious enough, then nothing truly would. In 2009, Madonna commented to Rolling Stone that she liked the song when she first heard the demo, because it was "ironic and provocative at the same time but also unlike me. I'm not a materialistic person..."

Anyone too outraged by the antics of Material Girl though, would have been pleased that Madonna could do the straight forward miming pop videos too. The mini film for her March 85 single Crazy For You was as straight forward as they come. The track was taken from the film Vision Quest, directed by Harold Becker, and the video itself consists of various scenes form the film in a rather corny montage style, interspersed with segments of Madonna's cameo in the movie, where she played a night club singer. It was standard stuff, but it did the job. There was a second video culled from the film's soundtrack too, the more upbeat and lesser known Gambler, and the promo once again consisted of scenes from the film.

The same year, Madonna released Into the Groove, the hit song included on the soundtrack of her first proper movie, Desperately Seeking Susan. Madonna had starred in a student film, A Certain Sacrifice, a few years earlier, but this kooky Hollywood comedy was her true debut as a film star. Playing a version of herself, the free spirited Susan entered film iconography almost instantly when the film became a big hit that year.

How did Madonna fit into the role of Susan? "Pretty much perfectly," the writer of the film, Leora Barish told me in 2015. "It fit her like a glove because it was kind of like her own bad-girl Boy Toy persona at the time, and on top of that, she rocked it. I think she especially connected with the amoral, pseudo criminal, selfish, powerful, curious, improvisational qualities of Susan. She's an accomplished, charismatic performer, but she's not really, you know, an actor. It's like a tune that she could play the shit out of. Like I said, she rocked it. She added her own riffs that revealed it, enhanced it, made it more saturated."

Even if you are not watching the film itself, the video presents so many nostalgic images from the film that it makes you want to grab it off the shelf and watch it all over again. One of those comforting 80s movies, Desperately Seeking Susan has stood the test of time; and so has the Into the Groove video for that matter, though it is very much beautifully within its time.

For many, Susan represented the zenith of Madonna's film career. Not requiring too much of a stretch, Madonna got by on charisma alone, and was magnetic on the screen, effortlessly walking away with the picture. In regards to Into the Groove, it is in many ways Madonna the icon at her most powerful; the song is wonderful, the film from which it was pulled is still a classic, and Madonna is here in all her legendary glory, in the outfit that millions of young girls all over the world adopted. Though the Into the Groove video is merely a montage of Madonna's moments in the movie, it still feels very much like its own entity.

The other Madonna video of 1985 (which really was her year) was Dress You Up, consisting of live footage from her first world tour,

The Virgin Tour. But she emerged in 1986 with a totally new look for a brand new video. The song came from her massive selling True Blue album. Live to Tell is one of her most tender and powerful ballads, and one of my personal favourite tracks from her whole career. Featuring a sturdy musical back drop, Madonna sings her heart out. It was recorded for the film At Close Range, directed by James Foley, and starring Madonna's then partner, the bad boy actor Sean Penn. The music itself had been created by Patrick Leonard for another film called Fire With Fire, but when Madonna heard the music as an instrumental she knew she had found the right backing for her next hit.

The video was directed by Foley himself, and in between scenes from the movie, we see a more stripped down, wholesome Madonna against a black back drop. Her hair was now in a wavy blonde style (very Monroe) and her make up more subtle, while the jewels of Material Girl and hedonistic outfits of Like A Virgin were replaced by a rather old fashioned, respectable flowered dress. She looked like a 1950s housewife, or at least a glamourised movie version of one. For Madonna, it was a totally new image, and here in 1986 the juxtaposition from Madonna the "it" girl of 1985 is staggering. Indeed, there has been a total transformation, and this understated Madonna fits not only for the video, but the song itself, perfectly. With a simple, restrained performance, Madonna takes us on an emotional journey with minimum effort. All our attention remains on Madonna and the real emotion the song harbours. Compared to the high camp performances on Material Girl, Like A Virgin and the earlier videos, this is pure class personified, proving that Madonna could devote herself to the song, the music, the feelings and the power, without distracting us with visual ironies and metaphors. Don't get me wrong, a Madonna on camp overload is certainly a lot of fun and can raise provocative issues and morals, but seeing her against a plain black screen, delivering the message of the song with purity and truth, is in a league of its own.

For Madonna, it was simply a way of changing things so she wouldn't get bored. It was the first significant change we had seen of her, and it worked. She proved early on that visual transformations would become everyday, and that her fans would not only accept these changes, but welcome them too. After all, nothing gets stale when it comes to Madonna.

"After a while I got sick of wearing tons of jewellery," she said to the New York Times, "I wanted to clean myself off. I see my new look as very innocent and feminine and unadorned. It makes me feel good. Growing up, I admired the kind of beautiful glamorous woman—from Brigitte Bardot to Grace Kelly—who doesn't seem to be around much anymore. I think it's time for that kind of glamour to come back. In pop music generally, people have one image. You get pigeonholed. I'm lucky enough to be able to change and still be accepted. If you think about it, that's what they do in the movies; play a part, change characters, looks and attitudes. I guess I do it to entertain myself."

The video was very important in ensuring that Madonna was free to have and adopt any image she felt like - the virgin, the man eater, the provocateur, the victim, the perpetrator etc. - and that the suits and big wigs would just have to accept it. Musically, the song was like nothing she had done before. She had done a cracking version of Love Don't Live Here Anymore on Like A Virgin, but this was the first ballad that really came from her. It required a fresh image, something as visually stark and honest as the emotive song. It proved just how valuable and important a single's accompanying video could be, and how Madonna could express herself in a whole new way, outside the confines of the three or four (in this case five) minute song. The video became an extension of her creativity, another outlet open for her to spread her wings within, and explore any and every avenue she felt drawn to.

For me, Live to Tell is one of Madonna's finest moments, both the song and video. Though this was a conscious change of image, it never for one-minute feels calculated or contrived. It comes across as sincere. At the time it surely must have surprised a hell of a lot of people. Madonna then, wasn't just the controversial pop star who pushed the sexual boundaries and pointed out the hypocrisy and sexist aspects for modern society. She was also a singer, pure and simple, capable of establishing an image while also making it purely about the song in question. As far as her acting goes, the Live to Tell video features some of her finest. It also helped make the song a Number 1 hit.

The True Blue album proved to be a real game changer for Madonna, both as a singer, an artist, a songwriter, and a video star. Live to Tell presented us with a new, more innocent Madonna, with none of the cavorting or writhing of her earlier work. And it didn't look forced either; nor did it even look like a character she had adopted.

As far as adopting characters went, Madonna was able to do so in her next video, getting under the skin of the part, resulting in one of

36

her best music video performances to date. The award winning Papa Don't Preach video was something else entirely. In many ways it was revolutionary and received much acclaim, with Madonna portraying a young woman telling her father, played by Danny Aiello, that she is pregnant and wants to keep the baby. It's a mini movie in itself, directed superbly (again, by the great James Foley) and performed well along to the exciting music. In America, it was seen as a controversial video, but 30 years on, while it's still provocative, it actually makes more sense in today's climate than ever before. The decision to keep the baby and not abort is certainly a powerful element for a supposed pop song and not a theme we would ever see raised in modern commercial music. Say what you will about her, Madonna was at least approaching the kind of controversial subject matter that no one else in the mainstream dared to.

The visual impact Madonna herself makes in the video cannot be exaggerated. If you span those two years or so since her true emergence, the changes in her are staggering, even at such an early stage. The punk haired disco queen of Everybody gave birth to the lusty street urchin of Burning Up and Borderline, while the leggings and tousled hair of Live A Virgin and the glamorous movie star of Material Girl led her into the respectable dress clad balladeer for Live to Tell. This makes the complete make over of Papa Don't Preach quite unbelievable. With short blond hair and a boyish look, Madonna becomes the teenage girl, despite being 27 at the time of filming. She gets so into the role that you might forget her past images (and songs), and take it as its own separate entry in her videography. Clearly, this is mini cinema, and even though the video runs no more than five minutes, Madonna has somehow fleshed out her character, and the troubled situation she is in, to such a degree that it feels like a fully formed, well rounded, multi faceted cinematic creation. She looks every bit the teenager in love, building up the courage to tell her passionate, fiery father the news. Like one would say of De Niro (again, I come back to the Method king himself) or any of the truly great actors, Madonna has become the character in every way. From the gum chewing, the coy romancing with her mechanic boyfriend, to the way she interacts with Aiello, it's a condensed film performance, well observed and executed. (And for the record, I still don't think Madonna gets enough credit for the richness of such bite sized characterisations.)

The video was shot over three days in Manhattan. Foley said that despite the serious message, the atmosphere was pure fun, with the crew blasting the song out full blast during filming.

"I was a bit spoiled because she had absolute creative freedom and could do whatever she wanted," recalled Foley. "We talked about wanting to tap into a working-class environment, because by that time she had done Material Girl and Like a Virgin and other stuff that was very glamorous and stylized. She wanted to do something a bit more grounded and drama. We took the script literally from the lyrics of the song, and I remember having a moment's hesitation about doing that because most videos are not literal interpretations. But I just felt like it was something that tied into her desire to dip into the working-class world. I did have the idea that there should be a segment of the video where she was Madonna — not the character in the story — and that's where it cuts to the black and white stuff of her dancing around for the chorus."

While videos like Material Girl had Madonna playing two beings, both were invented characters - the movie star wooed by the producer and the big screen character in the guise of Monroe. Here though, as Foley pointed out, there are two characters, but one is actually the singer we know as Madonna. In her recognisable, tight outfit and her dyed short blonde hair in the miming segment of the video, she is clearly Madonna the narrator, presenting to us the moral tale as it is. By following the flow of the lyrics and the story of the song itself, Foley and Madonna revolutionised the music video format. In this era, videos were usually close to their songs, maybe in a thematic style or by using allusions to the lyrics, but here the two go hand in hand totally. There is no visual trickery and no metaphors here; everything is told through the lyrics, and they are brought to life by the straight forward linear plot. It has to be said that while other big names at the time were doing great things with the pop video format (Michael Jackson's Thriller album boasted some classic pop single videos), none were tackling serious issues, the kind of which we normally read about in a novel or see in a an art house movie. Madonna was bringing the rather unglamorous problems people face out there in the real world not only to song, but also to the usually glitzy, largely escapist world of pop video. MTV had never seen something so brave.

"I've made a bunch of films and videos and it's one of the five things that I've done that I feel unequivocally good about," Foley told Rolling Stone. "The strongest thing I came away from was the value of creative freedom, and that she used that in a very smart way. She's extremely focused and mature and had a work ethic. It was a good lesson to me: what to do with absolute, creative power. She's respectful of people's jobs and sees herself where she fits into it very well. I always thought, whenever I get total final cut on the movie, I will remember how she handled that freedom."

Foley saw out his Madonna trilogy that same year, with the mega hit True Blue. More playful and staged than the previous two videos, True Blue was good lighthearted fun and nothing else. Visually, it was (like the song) a homage to the old girl singing groups, with Madonna and her backing dancers clearly having a lot of fun. Visually, it saw Foley playing repeatedly on the colour blue (blue backdrop, blue outfit) in the title, a visual treat that lacked any real message or meaning. And that was just fine, for it reflected the care free, loved up feel of the song itself. Madonna could deliver light popcorn pop better than anyone else, and once again took the opportunity to pay tribute to the golden days, in this case the bright and colourful rock and roll imagery of the 50s. Pop art gold.

In Jean Baptiste Mondino's video for Open Your Heart, also from 1986, Madonna returned to a more overtly sexual persona, only this one was different to the ones she had adopted in past videos. Here the dilemma for many viewers and observers (feminist or otherwise) was whether Madonna was empowering herself in order to poke fun at male voyeurism and the objectification of the female form, or merely providing thrills for the audience watching at home. Madonna believers will certainly go for the former, me included. In Open Your Heart, Madonna the Basque wearing exotic dancer in a peep show, writhing for the gawping males, is very much in command. The men are merciless, defenseless in the face of her seduction, and the fact they can look but can't touch is the biggest wind up of all. Madonna is turning the mirror on us all. When we watch her, and not just her, but all women objectified on TV, what do we get from the experience? The average sexist male can stare open mouthed, and the supposedly outraged can act shocked; but at the end of the day, it is Madonna's body, her being, and her choice. Essentially, she is her own entity. Whether people condemn, enjoy or objectify her is up to the individual. The important thing, I believe, is to be seen, and how each individual person is seeing and perceiving is irrelevant to the artistic choices someone like Madonna makes.

Videos today would be seedy if dealing with the star being a stripper, but from the word go, and the glimpse of blown up Tamara de Lempicka art above the entrance to the peep show, Open Your Heart is a classy affair. As the young boy enters the peep show, the first glimpse we see of Madonna is when the wall comes up, revealing her in her black basque, in a black char with a black wig on. She is channeling her inner Liza Minelli for sure, only with the sex factor turned up to eleven. When she removes her black wig, Madonna reveals her classic short True Blue hair do, slicked back, as she straddles the chair and gets her moves going.

Madonna is clearly enjoying herself putting on various personas, escaping into a fantasy world that were it not for the leering men through the flaps, would be a private haven; and if she ignores the faces out there, that is precisely what it could be. The little boy waiting for her outside represents innocence, something needed in the life of a woman who removes her clothes for money, for the entertainment of sleazy, dark eyed males. But the customers are just as blank faced and dead as the painted men, and the mannequins which stare on blankly. Madonna is the one who is truly alive and vital, the watchers merely existing, basking in her glow. The life of the peeper is unfulfilled. When they leave the peep show, they go to their lonely hovels. Madonna goes off arm in arm with the sweetness and naivety of youth, to dance and frolic in child like glee. The final image of Madonna and child, both in their suits and hats, heading off down the street in sweet silhouette, finishes off the video in style and beauty; one of the most enduring shots from her music video career.

"The set was built from scratch," Mondino recalled to Rolling Stone. "We found this place where we could actually build it. We just built the front of it and the little booth where the old man was inside. I guess it was my Hollywood period where I was in a Hollywood state of mind with my cranes, the building... We were very young [*laughs*] and everything was possible, I guess. I like the fakeness of it. I haven't seen it for a long time, but when I saw it once again, I said, "It's so naïve." It's kind of badly done, which I like, compared to today. We didn't have the same equipment, people are more skilful today, but there's something sweet about it. I love the ending; like a Charlie Chaplin ending when they run after each other. That little moment is very touching."

This was Madonna's first overtly sexualized video, it has to be said. Yes, Like A Virgin had certainly been provocative, but Madonna hadn't really shed her clothing and challenged the male attitudes dead on until this. But her performance didn't and still doesn't come across as pointless gratuity, or semi nudity for the sake of it; it is clearly a daring and bold statement, holding the mirror to us all - and perhaps up to herself too. Culled from her True Blue album, the single was released in November of 1986, her last release of the year, and a top ten hit the world over.

Madonna teamed up with Mary Lambert again for the video for La Isla Bonita, Madonna's tribute to the Latin Americans. The song did most of the selling, but the video remains visually arresting. In a beautiful red dress, looking every bit the classic beauty, Madonna advanced upon her street images from previous videos and became a glamorous icon worthy of movie star status. As Latin faces dance around her (I always love the sight of the old man with the two carrier bags) Madonna remains the focal point, expressing herself majestically, especially in the tearful bedroom scenes where she peers through the curtain. Madonna adopts two personas, the fun loving cavorter in the red dress and the pensive, meditative, heavy eyed watcher in white vest and slicked back hair. Freda Kahlo comes to mind, and once again Madonna explores the duality of the modern woman, the dreamer and the dream in one package. Though some felt Madonna's depictions of the Latin Americans bordered on stereotypes, others found the video affectionate and respectful.

For her 1987 video Who's That Girl?, a single plucked from the film of the same name (a critical and commercial disappointment, but more of that later), Madonna teamed up with director Peter Rosenthal for a fairly straight forward promo clip. Interspersed with bits of the movie, the video thread has Madonna dressed in grey with short black hair and a hat, miming to the track and messing around in a park with two kids. One of the lesser videos from this era, it does the job that most music films did in this era - it sells the song, pure and simple.

Two years later with the release of her masterpiece LP Like A Prayer, Madonna's videos seemed to become even more accomplished, not so much promos but movies in their own right, cramming as much cinematic and dramatic range into their limited time spans as possible, without ever feeling fussy or over stuffed.

While the videos for songs such as Like A Virgin and Material Girl had got the tongues wagging, the film for Like A Prayer caused outrage and shock. With its "Black Jesus" iconography, not to mention the burning crosses and the fact she actually kisses her Christ figure, the video caused quite a stir. Pepsi, who had been sponsoring Madonna at the time, removed the song from their latest ad. Madonna's reply? "Art should be controversial and that's all there is to it." There is much truth in the statement, and that one sentence could be adopted as her official mantra.

In the video, we see a brunette Madonna (a dark haired Madge usually means it's going to be pretty serious, or that she means business) witness a murder, for which a black man gets wrongfully arrested. The real killers give Madonna a menacing, threatening look and she instantly knows she can't speak out the truth for her own safety. She goes to the church and prays to a black figurine of Jesus, which later comes to life. She enjoys an erotic moment with him and comes to the realisation that she needs to speak out and tell the police that the black man is innocent. When the man is released, Madonna has reached a certain moral revelation, a zenith of understanding. As the choir embraces and welcomes her, she dances in sheer glee, as if born again.

Even if you are "offended" by the imagery (Lord knows why anyone really should be) you can't argue with the strength of the concept, and how clever Madonna was getting in combining religion and sex, faith and passion. When we see Madonna dancing before the burning crosses, it brings to mind the sickening racism of the KKK, and when

44

she is kissed by the Christ figure (played by Leon Robinson) one cannot deny the power. As provocative as it clearly was for such a staunchly religious America, the video raises interesting issues and is masterfully crafted and shot. Although it's predictable to note, it's a movie condensed into five minutes, completely whole as its own entity, with or without the song. It just so happens that the song itself is a masterpiece; but even without it, the video's messages are loud and clear.

Director Mary Lambert later spoke of the controversial video: "I knew that we were pushing some big buttons, but I sort of underestimated the influence and bigotry of fundamentalist religion and racism in this country and the world. I always think that, if my work is successful, it goes beyond my intentions and in this case it definitely did. The most important thing was to force people to reimagine their visual references and really root out their prejudices. Using burning crosses to reference racism to religion. Why not a Black Jesus? Why can't you imagine kissing him? I wanted to speak about ecstasy and to show the relationship between sexual and religious ecstasy. I think that subconsciously a lot of people understood this and were either enthralled or outraged by it. Consciously, I don't think a lot of the audience would have made this interpretation."

The video for Express Yourself lacked the controversy of Like A Prayer, but was just as momentous and cinematic a piece of filmmaking. Looking every bit the gorgeous and glamorous star, Madonna appears majestically in a Metropolis homage directed by David Fincher, a video which was very much her baby and her vision.

"This one I had the most amount of input," Madonna later recalled. "I oversaw everything—the building of the sets, everyone's costumes, I had meetings with make-up and hair and the cinematographer, everybody. Casting, finding the right cat—just every aspect. Kind of like making a little movie. We basically sat down and just threw out all every idea we could possibly conceive of and of all the things we wanted. All the imagery we wanted—and I had a few set ideas, for instance the cat and the idea of Metropolis. I definitely wanted to have that influence, that look on all the men—the workers, diligently, methodically working away."

A true film in every way, the video (though calling it a video underwrites its power in my view) remains one of the most stunning and consistently powerful Madonna videos of the 1980s and beyond. As the powerful figure, Madonna reverses the male role and stands high as the leader of this futuristic land, a true feministic image which established her as the powerful modern woman more than any other of her videos ever did. On a budget of 5 million dollars, Madonna and Fincher perhaps crafted the finest - at least on a technical level - video of the 1980s. In many ways it illustrates how good music video could, and hopefully still can be, and remains the zenith of the more exuberant and indulgent side of the art form.

One of her most tasteful, moving and classy videos also came from the Like A Prayer album, also directed by Fincher. The song was Oh Father and it featured some striking visuals, with a cropped Madonna in black at her moody best. Mixing autobiographical details with fiction based on a relationship between a father and daughter (possibly or possibly not Madonna and her own dad), the song is still one of her most powerful pieces, and its accompanying video more than measures up to its stature. It also features some pretty disturbing sights, like the girl going to her mother's coffin and seeing her mother's lips sewn up. The fact this was based on Madonna's own memories makes the video even more unsettling, but also more beautiful and truer than any of her other videos.

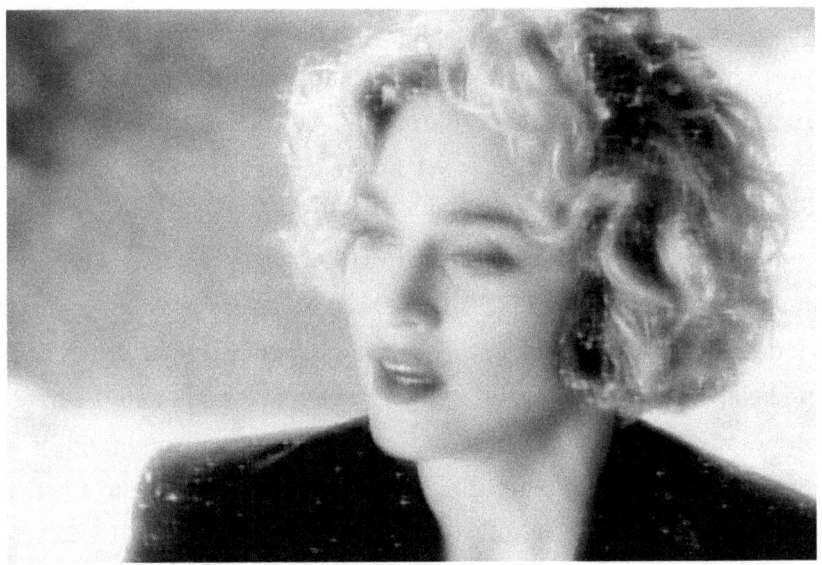

Oh Father.

Even as she redefined the music video and blitzed through the Like A Prayer singles with innovative movies, she proved she could also make simple ones; like, for instance, her video for Cherish. While Madonna has since called the song kind of goofy, it's a lovely, warm and bubbly love-pop song, and features an equally unfussy and unpretentious video of Madonna, looking great in black, cavorting on a beach - and getting increasingly wetter as she does so. It was rather

47

straight forward, especially in the wake of Express Yourself, but it proved she was no one trick pony.

Twenty years later, Lady Gaga emerged and took on similarly huge video extravaganzas as these, but while she pushed boundaries with far out films for songs like Bad Romance, the music rarely matched the visuals - and once Gaga had done the truly outrageous a few times again and again, backed by straight forward pop, there was nowhere else to go. In many ways, Madonna's videos reached their mightiest in size and budget in this era, and in the 1990s she would prove herself with smaller, lower budget, more arty videos, like the ones for Human Nature, Take A Bow, Secret, and perhaps most memorably of all, Justify My Love. By going smaller after the massive budgets of the Like A Prayer era, Madonna proved her worth, and the fact she did not need buckets of money, visual distractions and elaborate sets to impress her audience - at least not all the time - in her music videos said a lot for her songs. But that run of videos in the glowing glory of the 1980s, from Everybody through to Cherish (let's not forget the childlike animated delights of Dear Jessie too) remain unmatched by any other artist who was out at the time or has come since. Even Michael Jackson could not measure up to her imagination, innovation and star quality. It's all there in the videos; but more importantly, it's all there in the music too.

SPECIAL EDITION: VIDEO '85

Music

Vol. IX, No. 7 March 28-April 10

(outside California $2.00) $1.50

THE MAKING OF MADONNA'S "MATERIAL GIRL"

MARY LAMBERT:
Rockvid's Hottest New Director

THE NEW SWITCHEROO:
Movie Directors Make Videos, Video Directors Make Movies

Plus:
Philip Bailey
The Tubes
U2
The Unforgiven

MC GUIDE TO VIDEO PROD. EQ.'S
L.A. VIDEO REPORT
Production, Programming, Labels

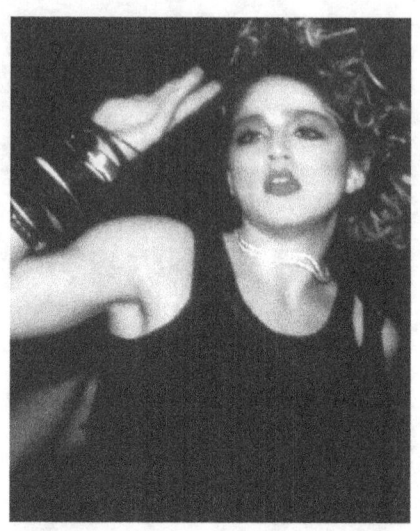

GEORGE DU BOSE
ON PHOTOGRAPHING
EARLY MADONNA

George Du Bose is an acclaimed photographer who got the chance to photograph Madonna in New York right at the start of her singing career in the early 1980s, when she was in The Breakfast Club group, even before the recording of her first album. Here he answers some questions about the embryonic queen of pop.

What were you doing at the time just before you came across Madonna?

I was a young photographer just finishing my apprenticeship to fashion photographers and my bosses allowed me to use their Nikons to go to nightclubs and document the New Wave music scene that was blowing up in Manhattan. I had photographed the NYC debut concerts for many bands and musicians; The B-52's, Kid Creole and the Coconuts, Joe Jackson, Klaus Nomi and many others. I was well-known at most of the trendy clubs, Max's Kansas City, CBGB's, the Mudd Club, Hurrah's and was either on the band's guest list or the doormen knew me and allowed me entry anyway.

John Phillips was the legendary doorman/bouncer at Hurrah's and a good pal of mine. He was also doing record promotion to radio stations as a day job and had recommended me to Camille Barbone, who was Madonna's first manager. Camille phoned me and although I had no idea who she was, she told me that she wanted me to go to Roslyn, NY, to a club called Uncle Sam's Blues and photograph the singer of a band (unnamed). She didn't want the rest of the band photographed at all, just the singer... I told Camille that my fee was $250 plus film, processing and train fare from Manhattan out to Roslyn, NY.

What about the gig itself? What songs did she play, do you remember? Was it a good set?

Her band was good, her performances were full of energy. In my book, "Madonna Raw", I have a photo of her set list that was lying on the stage by her microphone stand. It is readable. I don't know if any of the songs that were performed in either of her sets that night made it to her first LP. Of course it was a good set or we wouldn't be talking about her today...

Actually, there were two sets with a break in the middle. It is during that middle break that I went backstage and found her sitting alone in the dressing room. I asked her what her name was and she replied, "Madonna." I asked what her real name was and she said, "Madonna." I told her that the outfit that she wore during her first set was pretty sexy and her performance was pretty sexy, but that she seemed nervous. I just told her that it was all "working". Camille heard me speaking to her and yelled at me, "Get out, get out! How dare you speak to my artist like that!" I went back to the concert room and photographed the second set.

Did you recognise much star quality in her? Was it evident at all?

I was observing the rise of many artists in the New Wave genre, which was a pretty broad and diverse field. I saw the beginning of many bands' careers. I began to get a sense of what bands got recording contracts and what paths these bands followed to break out in the US. Madonna had "star" written all over...

She looked drastically different from the Madonna we all came to know. Do you think she had a long way to go from there or do you think it was all there underneath and just needed tuning?

From the photos in "Madonna Raw" it is clear that for the first set she wore a black leather miniskirt and black leather top. This outfit reminded me of "Jane" in the Johnny Weissmueller "Tarzan" films from the 1930s. The second set, it is clear that Madonna does a "strip" from a marching band leader's coat, to a sweater with the University of Michigan, then the sweater was off, revealing a white man's dress shirt. Clearly, Madonna was in need of a fashion consultant and was searching for her "look".

At some point prior to the photoshoot for her first album cover, she met Maripol, a French jewellery designer living in Manhattan. Maripol got Madonna to wear rubber jewellery and the crucifix that was influential during her early career. I don't think Madonna ever gave Maripol props for the contribution that she made to Madonna's career.

In what way was she sexy? Can you describe it at all?

The outfit from her first set was certainly sexy in a jungle-look way. Her stage demeanour, rolling around on stage, clearly showed that she was "into" her performance and was just "letting it all hang out". She certainly was cute in a punky way and presented a "rebel with a cause" persona.

From that small experience, why is it that she seems to have bewitched so many people? In that instance did you get any insights into her appeal to get people hooked?

At that early concert that I photographed in Roslyn, I wasn't paying any attention to the audience's reaction. I don't recall that there were more than twenty people in attendance. The next show I saw was on the roof of Danceteria, a club in Manhattan. There were many people on the roof that night, whether they were there to see Madonna or for the grilled hamburgers, I am not sure, but now Madonna was singing and dancing to recordings. There was no band. Her brother and another woman were dancing along with her.

I had brought Yuki Watanabe and Michael O'Brien to the Danceteria event. These two gentlemen were promoting Manhattan's rising stars one night a month in a Boston nightclub. The monthly event was called New York 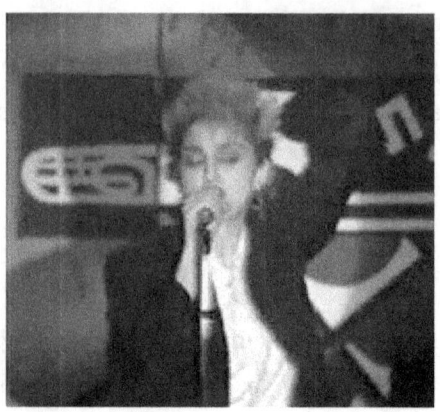 Nights. They made a three camera video shoot of her concert, again to dance tracks accompanied by her brother and another female dancer. There was a large crowd at her Boston debut, but the audience may have just come to see "who was new", never hearing of Madonna before. Madonna was now wearing her new "Maripol" look.

Madonna has refused to release the video that was produced that night. There are snippets of it on YouTube. Camille Barbone was so miffed that I had spoken to her artist, that she never collected the contact sheets from that first night and I never got paid...

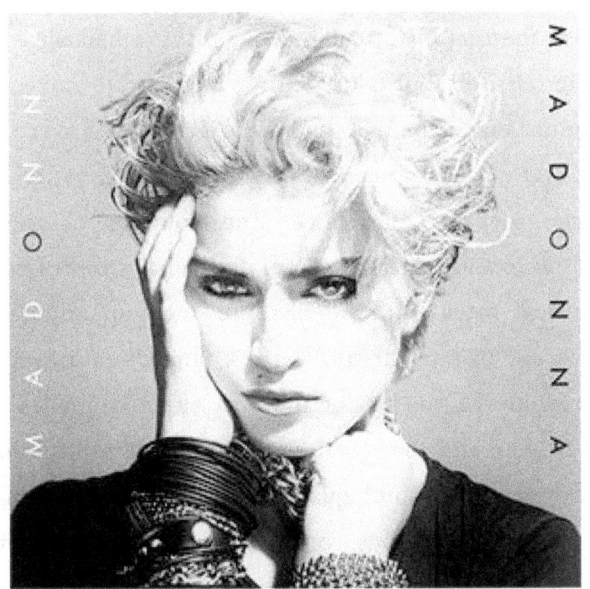

THE FIRST ALBUM
A DETAILED RE-ANALYSIS

"My inspiration is simply that I love to dance. All I wanted to do was make a record that I would want to dance to, and I did. Then I wanted to go one step further and make a record that people would listen to on the radio."

Like Paul McCartney symbolically counting in the 1960s on The Beatles' I Saw Her Standing There, the first track on their Please Please Me album, in many ways the first spiralling synths of Madonna's Lucky Star, the opener of her debut LP, kick started the 1980s in a very similar way. OK, so this sounds a little over the top. After all, the world was three years into this new decade already, and on top of numerous historical incidents, there had also been some great music released. But take a closer look and it makes sense. The death of John Lennon in 1980 had put a dark cloud over the musical landscape, and what was needed, perhaps, was a sense of fun, a slice of child-like glee to blow away the cobwebs of the arguably underwhelming seventies. For some, the eighties represent the death of the musical artist and the birth of the yuppie infested, mass consumerist age of mainstream shallow pop. Of course, it isn't all so black and white. Music production was at its height in the 1980s, especially in pop, and though the quality of the music didn't always match the top notch sound quality and sonic innovations whirling around in those heady times, some of the music transcended the art form itself.

The year of 1983 was a mixed one, and all these years on, a scroll through the list of releases shows that very few have lasted the subsequent decades and come out as timeless records. Bands like The Stranglers and Dire Straits, survivors of the punk and new wave era, were putting out their weakest material, while new talent seemed rather thin on the ground. The icons of the previous two decades looked like spent forces around this time too; Lou Reed's Legendary Hearts was shameful in comparison to his early 70s glory years, while The Kinks and Pink Floyd's new work was a shadow of what had come before.

And there, released two days after Metallica's debut thrash metal classic Kill Em All, and on the very same day as Neil Young's jokey but lacking Everybody's Rockin', was a self titled LP by a new female singer called Madonna. Keep glancing through that year, and there are very few female artists releasing work; and the ones that are there were mostly already veterans, like Bette Midler, Carly Simon and Joan Jett. Of course, Cyndi Lauper would hit the charts with her own debut record later that same year - in October in fact, with She's So Unusual - but otherwise it was a stale time for the women.

The success of Madonna was not instant though. After all, she had already released two singles from the LP the previous year (Everybody and Burning Up) and it would take a few months before it started to seriously sell. But the LP had arrived, and so had Madonna, and she could not have come at a more vital time.

We all know it took Madonna a few years to get to the point where her name graced an album cover, and though her rise to fame is interesting, it has been written about many times before. This article really hopes to pin point the magic of the music she gave us on that fabulous debut, which I feel has been pushed aside over the years in favour of her bigger selling follow ups - and of course her public image.

Madonna struggled through the early 80s making just enough to survive, popping up in art films and working as a backing dancer for lesser talents. She also mixed with a lot of musicians in the New York music scene, all of whom taught her valuable lessons for the future. "They taught me chord progressions," she recalled, "so I could start writing songs straight away. I was full of energy and raring to go! I was also in some 16 millimetre art movies, no story, just images chopped up to make you think about things. I was doing all sorts of wacky things, screaming and running around changing costumes; having monologues with myself talking to the camera. There was another more narrative one, a love story. I was the lead girl, it was real stupid, I was this S and M girl, a dominatrix, and I had these slaves. It was really hilarious!"

Clearly Madonna was searching for her outlet, trying anything and everything which came her way in hope of some kind of miraculous discovery. By 1982, Madonna was seriously attempting a career in music. She had a band, The Breakfast Club, who adopted a more hard rocking sound to what she would take on in her solo records. The band nearly got a record deal, but after Madonna wanted to lead them in a more funky direction, they were dropped. Clearly, the Breakfast Club were going nowhere, at least not in the direction or speed Madonna wanted them to.

After shedding the group and deciding to go out alone as a solo star, Madonna got a decent contract with Sire Records, when the label president Seymour Stein had been impressed by Madonna's songs. He signed her for two singles first, and when Everbody became a dance hit, she was given an album deal. Working alongside Warner Bros. producer Reggie Lucas, he encouraged her to go full pop, and the pair cut a stonking, commanding version of Burning Up together. Then they began to build up more songs, with a view of titling their record Lucky Star after one of the strongest tracks they had in their arsenal.

Displeased with the way some of the recording was going, Madonna brought in John "Jellybean" Benitez to re-jig the whole production. To Madonna, Lucas was pushing her out and not accepting her ideas, diminishing her input and piling on too many sounds which only did disservice to the songs. Benitez remixed the songs and generally updated it to what Madonna had in mind.

58

"She was unhappy with the whole album," Jellybean Benitez later said, "so I went in and sweetened up a lot of music for her, adding some guitars to Lucky Star, some voices, some magic... I just wanted to do the best job I could do for her. When we would playback Holiday or Lucky Star, you could see that she was overwhelmed by how great it all sounded. You wanted to help her, you know? As much as she could be a bitch, when you were in groove with her, it was very cool, very creative."

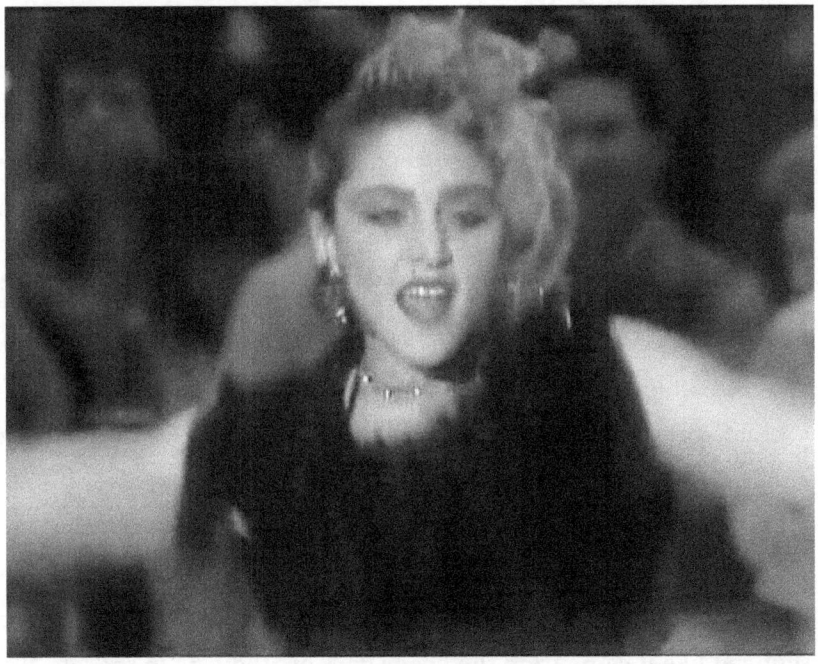

Upon the record's release, Madonna was calling her music "soul pop", and she explained her reasons behind that tag to Island Magazine in October, a few months after the LP was released, now selling well and establishing her fame. "Because I have soul," she said, pretty much telling the readers that this music was all about her and her spirit, her passion, her untameable wildness. "Because you can dance to it. Cause you can, you know. I grew up in an all black neighbourhood and I wanted to be a black girl. I really did. There was something about me that was so much freer than the white kids I knew and they didn't go to the Catholic schools I went to. They went to other schools and they wore short dresses and they didn't have to take baths all the time and their knees were always dirty. I liked the fact that they could braid their hair and it would be sticking up... that's not why I'm braiding my hair right now. First of all, all the black girls in my neighbourhood had these dances in their yard where they had these little turntables with 45 records and they'd play all this Motown stuff and they would dance, just dance, all of them dancing together and none of the white kids I knew would ever do that. They were really boring and stiff. And I wanted to be part of the dancing. I didn't like my friends. I had to be beaten up so many times by these little black girls before they would accept me and finally one day they whipped me with a rubber hose till I was like, lying on the ground crying. And then they just stopped doing it all of a sudden and let me be their friend, part of their group."

That Madonna had ever wanted to be a "part" of any group and not the leader of it seems unbelievable today, but this anecdote is vital in understanding Madonna's take on pop in 1983. At times, the music sounded like it came from the heady days of Studio 54 in the late 70s, and her slant on disco started a whole new movement in mid 80s pop. After the album became a hit, Madonna was established as a role model and fashion icon to girls all over the world. Her image was plastered on every bedroom wall and Madonna was name of the moment. But at the end of the day, how many people were really discussing the music? We all know Madonna became the Queen of Pop and dominated MTV for the whole decade to follow, but I feel the music is so often unfairly stepped over, often treated as a side note to her massive fame and success.

To the Madonna of 1983, this new brand of disco was just what was needed in the vacuous pop landscape, and she saw that her music had real substance, not just a shiny exterior and a danceable beat. "Most dance records now are just sounds, they're not songs that go with the group that go with the feeling that go with the fashion," she said. "I think that was the whole downfall of disco – that it didn't represent anything to anyone. It's changing slowly but you still have to eventually get away from the disco circuit to be taken seriously, or have any kind of a long life. I didn't realize how crucial it was for me to break out of the disco mould before I'd nearly finished the album. I wish I could have got a little more variety in there. The musicians were all guys who are making a thousand dollars a day in the studio so we couldn't rehearse much. Halfway through we all started doubting each other."

Despite this, the music was fresh and exciting at the time of release, and it has to be said that though people say the LP was a blueprint and Madonna herself called the songs rather weak, it still sounds fantastic to this day, as new and bubbling with energy as ever before. It's partly down to the production - no doubt about that - but in the truest sense the success of the LP is in the song writing. After all, had the album sounded good but had lousy, so-so, forgettable songs, it surely would not have catapulted her to success. While they were being mesmerised by her look and image, they were also being charmed by the music, whether they really knew so or not.

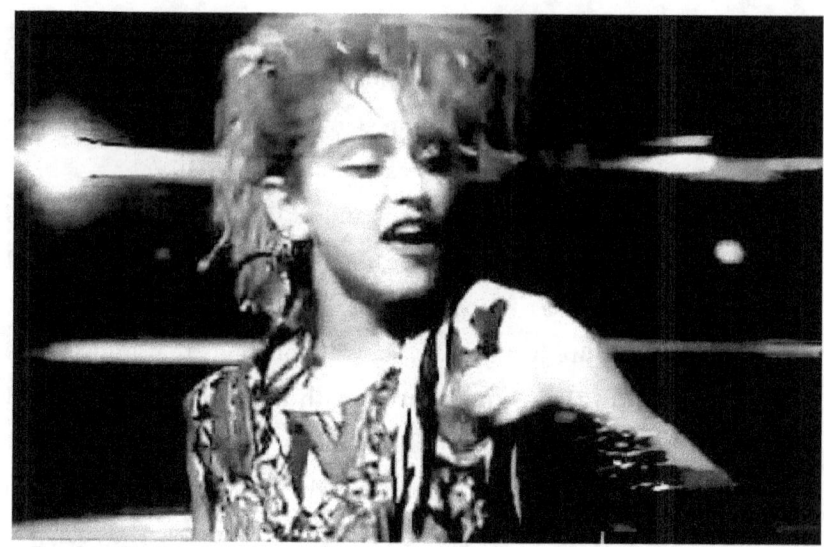

Lucky Star opens the album in true style, establishing the mood and vibe of the next forty minutes and eight tracks. The album feels like a party you've been lucky enough to get an invite to, and it never lets up its sense of fun, glee and energy, not for a single second. "It's all about escapism," she said to Interview Magazine, defining what her music was all about. "To make people forget about the problems of the world. It's just to cheer people up. People go out to dance to get away and forget about their problems, like a holiday, and that's what the music's about - to get together and forget."

Like much of the record, there is an innocence and sweetness to Lucky Star, its bubbling synths and solid beats making room for a high pitched, charismatic and appealing vocal performance by Madonna, who sounds more alive than she ever has in the song's 5 and a half minutes. The drums are chunky and make up the meat of the arrangement, while there are imaginative flourishes all the way through the mix. It's a massively rich production for a simplistic pop record, with a sturdy power bass, funky guitars and duelling keyboards filling out the gaps.

Remarkably Madonna did not want to release Lucky Star as a single, but record executive Jeff Ayeroff convinced her to do so. It became the fourth single released from the album, after Holiday, and became a wide hit, essentially getting her out into the world. If this were your first exposure to Madonna, it would no doubt get you firmly hooked and pulled in. There is an addictive quality to the song, and it feels, even today, like a wind of fresh air coming into the room. In short, it makes you feel happy. If Madonna was after giving her listeners light escapism, Lucky Star achieved that more than any other track.

The LP's second song, Borderline, was another single, released just after Lucky Star as the album's fifth stand alone release. It proved to be an even bigger hit than Lucky Star, basically giving her even wider exposure. Musically, Borderline has a strange mix of joy and slight melancholia, present in its weaving melodies and Madonna's longing vocal performance. Accompanied by a superb video which had Madonna as a model torn between her new fast life style as a photographer's subject and her more modest boyfriend, the track sold Madonna as a music and visual star, someone to listen to intently but also "look" at in the very purest sense. She established herself as a true force early on.

For many, Borderline was "it", the moment of Madonna's true arrival. Within the context of the rest of the album, with no visuals or commentary on her life and career at that point in time (February 1984 when it was released as a single), the song is another prime cut on a very enjoyable record, and it has its own special magic and glow. It proves how good this music is, that thirty five years later it works on its own level, divorced from the goings on of the mid 1980s and far removed from the excitement of Madonna's aura in that time. Borderline is solid gold pop, and though the lyrics have a troubled air, Madonna's vocals are genuine and heartfelt, while the music is even richer than it is on Lucky Star.

At the time, this was clearly seen by many as something very special, a whole package of song and pop star. The man who signed Madonna, Seymour Stein, said as much years later to Rolling Stone. ""I dared to believe this was going to be huge beyond belief, the biggest thing I'd ever had, after I heard Borderline. The passion that she put into that song, I thought there's no stopping this girl."

Producer Reggie Lucas also spoke of the song, but revealed more of its composition and recording. "Borderline has a stylistic similarity to Never Knew Love Like This Before [Stephanie Mills song that Lucas co-wrote and co-produced], particularly in the front, with Dean Gant's electric piano introduction. This was the first record I ever used a drum machine instead of a drummer. And the bass on Borderline is an ARP 2600 synthesizer, but the great Anthony Jackson – who did that intro on the O'Jays' For the Love of Money – is playing along on an electric bass guitar, and they're playing so tight you can't tell the difference."

Lucas has a point. Thirty five years on and one of the words which comes to mind here is "tight". There is a unity to the sound which is both infectious and seamless. It's so completely formed together as a unit that you do not stop and think of each musical "ingredient" so to speak, but the sound as a whole. It's like one united cluster of feelings and emotions, wonderfully played, but most of all, majestically sung by Madonna. Without her electric vocal, the song would merely be a nice instrumental.

Burning Up remains one of Madonna's most urgent, highly sexually charged and vital songs, recently revived live in the form of a hard rocker on the 2015 Rebel Heart Tour (just listen to the version on the accompanying live album, with Madonna on a flying V guitar, calling the crowd "Motherfuckers"!), but here in a much more primal, new wave, post punk form. Beginning with a punchy drum beat, the song bursts to life with a catchy bass line playing side by side with a synth (the chords are perfect here) and occasional guitars adding subtle power. Again though, it is Madonna's voice which grabs you by the scruff of the neck and commands you to sit up. As a lusty declaration of her burning passion, few could have hoped to match this back in the mid 1980s; and when accompanied by its sexy video, the song makes a case for Madonna being the most captivating pop star of the day. On its own, without the distractions of Madonna rolling about in the middle of an empty road, it remains one of her finest cuts, a delicious slice of rock-pop, packing a meaty punch and giving the listener another (third so far) shade of Madonna, at the time an emerging force on the charts.

Burning Up went back to Madonna's earlier years, when it was on the demo tape with Everybody and Ain't No Big Deal which she carried around with her and famously gave to DJ Mark Kamins, who get her a deal with Sire. The original demo is good, but it lacks the punch and instant grab of the album version. Burning Up was released as a single in March of 1983. It did not become a hit single, despite a nice release campaign and plenty of promo appearances, but did get on the Dance Club Singles Chart. These days, it's hard to see why the song was not a hit. Retrospectively, it's just as strong (in my view, stronger in fact) as the more iconic songs from the first album, and the punk energy gives it an extra boost. Perhaps though, it's down to the starker and sparser arrangement. After all, the pop buyers of 83 and 84 wanted colourful sounds, and Madonna gave them that on Lucky Star and Borderline, which were much brighter and full of exuberance. Burning Up, though, was spare in comparison (moody synths, bass and the odd bit of guitar), and Madonna's desire was so intense that perhaps some parents decided not to buy it for their kids. Indeed, there is a sense of desperation to her voice here, the fact she openly admits she is not like the others and will do "anything". It seems that even this early on in the game, Madonna knew she was willing to go all the way, musically and artistically, and indeed would do just that in later years (I'm thinking the early 90s here, definitely her most "shocking" era).

I Know It is the most quintessentially 80s track here, with punchy, echoey drums and perky keyboards dominating the mix. Madonna's voice is open and engaging, while the melody she sings is simplicity personified. The verses have a light air about them, while sadness and fear sneaks in for the chorus, with Madonna sure that this man is going to leave her. The weight of the chorus contrasts wonderfully with the optimism of the music in the verses, while Madonna becomes more bitter and regretful as the song goes on.

For years I have seen I Know It as one of the album's weakest cuts, and rather inconsequential compared to the more famous songs surrounding it. But the older I get the more I appreciate its approach, its tone and style. It is clearly more of a challenging song, and compared to the more approachable singles which adorn this record like jewels on a crown, it can seem like lesser fare. It is, in fact, a very cleverly constructed slice of pop, fooling you into a false sense of security. Indeed, it sounds like a positive, loved up power cut, but it's a song of intense longing and insecurity. The music, full of minor chords, bleeps and endless shuffling drums, is relentless, pained and frantic, mirroring the emotions of the dissatisfied singer of the song. One could be forgiven for overlooking the song (I did for years actually), but when one stops and actually realises what it achieves on this other wise completely positive, "overjoyed" album, you can appreciate it. There is also a nice bit of sax in there too.

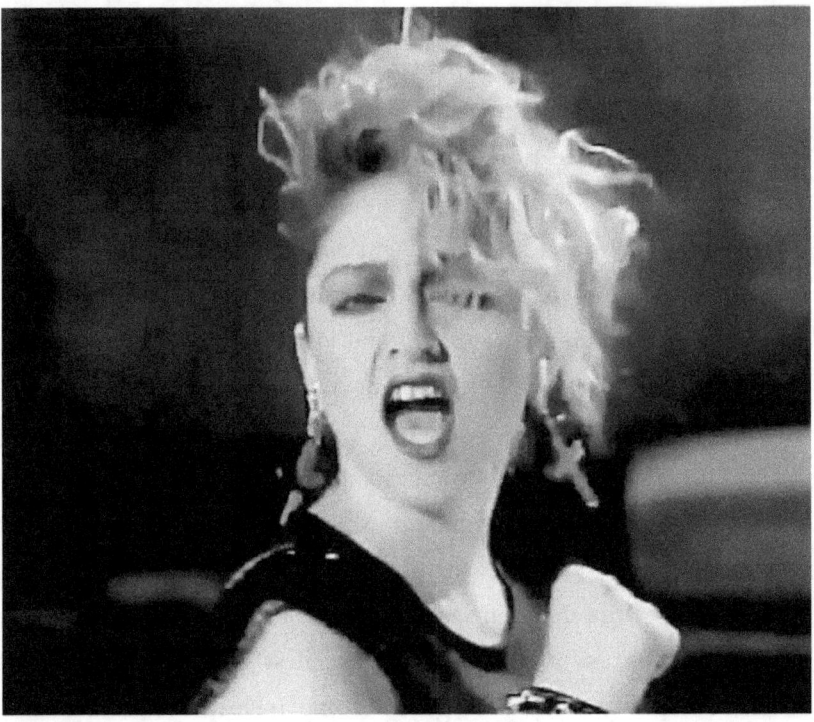

Holiday is much simpler, more straight forward and possibly the most care free track on the record. Plucked from a song by Curtis

Hudson and Lisa Stevens by Jellybean, it was Fred Zarr who gave the song its bounce and magic when he took the song and made an electronic arrangement. Madonna recorded her vocals and Jellybean then worked on the production to give the song the bounce and commercial appeal it has today.

Today there is something rather moving about the song's wide eyed sense of fun, it naivety and purity. The way the music bounces is really quite infectious, while the bass line and keyboards work wonderfully together. Madonna's vocals are as innocent as they ever would be, and the sense of fun is utterly magical. Madonna's message would never be so pure again, and in later years, perhaps some of us might long for such simple dance fare once again. For me though, the song is so of its time that it remains permanently fixed there, and if Madonna ever tried to recapture it, it just wouldn't be right. She is an artist who needs to keep moving, developing and enhancing her own sense of self, and Holiday, I am sure, feels so far away to her these days it's almost as if it's sung by a different person in a different life. The joy of Madonna's musical and visual timeline is that it is so varied, and Holiday, while still being enjoyable, belongs firmly in that era.

Think of Me is musically punchy and chunky, mixed solidly and evenly well. The drums are driven, while the bass and synth combo packs a real punch (especially on the up close intimacy of the headphones) while the frenzied verses lead to the pay off, the subtle but hooky chorus. It's one of the simplest songs here, and the message is pretty clear. This guy is going to lose her if he doesn't buck up his ideas and pull his finger out. Again, it's Madonna calling out for attention from the man of the song who disrespects her so;

and to we the listener, who cannot help but sit up to attention and get pulled into the irresistible beats and rhythms.

At this stage Madonna is not the lyrical melody master she would become only a couple of albums later (her vocal melodies are always so imaginative, especially in her weightier ballads), but her voice has a richness and honesty about it that wins you over, even when the melodies are basic. Physical Attraction could be seen as lesser Madonna, but it is musically very enticing (some great guitar lines going on in this song) and Madonna is lusty once again, waiting for her lover to arrive and "stay the night". The clever thing here is that Madonna is not begging the man to stay forever and commit to her with his eternal love. She clearly adds that if he stays the night and leaves in the morning she won't mind. This song is about sexual chemistry, the magnetism that is impossible to resist, and stays away from talk of love and destiny. Musically, it just gets richer, especially in the middle eight section where the keyboards weave wonderful melodies around Madonna's sexually charged lyrics.

The album ends with a true classic Madonna cut, the magnificent Everybody. A six minute ode to dance and letting loose, the song starts with a frenzied keyboard line over a shuffling dance beat. Madonna steps forward and delivers a sexy, breathy introduction inviting the man who has been watching and waiting to come on the dance floor and let loose with her. The song says little else, but as a tribute to the dance floor and the temptations and satisfactions it holds, the song cannot be bettered. The music is wonderfully played and put together too.

Everybody was one of the first famous Madonna songs, and she had demoed it with Steve Bray in 1982, it being on the tape she handed to the DJ Mark Kamins in the club. Released in October of 1982, it put the time span of the single releases up to a year and a half, illustrating how much Sire really wanted to push her. As a philosophy, Everybody neatly encapsulates everything Madonna's world was about in the years 1982, 83 and even 84 and beyond. It was about dancing, letting go, doing your thing and not caring about what anyone - in Madonna's case the rest of the world - thinks.

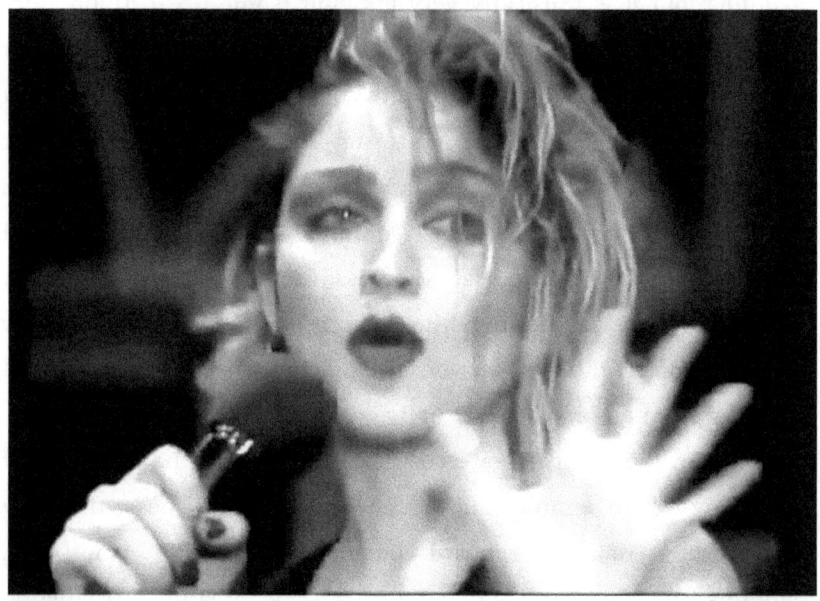

There's an infectious joy to these songs, a simplicity that takes you back to your own younger years when music was music for the sake of it, and you did not over analyse or look deeper for messages and truths. If this record, closing with the anthemic Everybody, does not make you feel happy, then you might just be a sorry individual.

There is an air of righteousness that makes it the most open and bare of all Madonna's albums. She was not yet a fully developed musical artist, and that's clear from the way she guides us through this un-cynical, light and breezy celebration of life itself. If this was Madonna as the New York street urchin put to vinyl, it was only her first role of the 1980s. To Island Magazine that year, she gave us an early clue about her ability to adopt other people's character traits, and also their looks, however consciously or subconsciously it might be done, to make a mutation all of her own. "I do feel really transient in a way," she said. "I feel like when I meet people I can absorb their character and be them. And I find that no matter what I'm doing I'm always doing the same thing. Basically. What ever it looks like on the outside. And it just makes me feel... I don't know, I can't really describe it verbally because no one's ever asked me this before, no one really cares. Haha! People just want to hear me sing."

That last line, 'people just want to hear me sing,' would not be true for much longer. Indeed, after her debut and into her second album and beyond, it seems that her singing was the last thing on many people's lists. It was all about Madonna the creation, the man eater, the ego maniac, the sex symbol. And for all her fame and success in the next couple of years, just as much negative stuff was written about her as it was positive, perhaps more so. She would become the target for all of society's ills, blamed for everything that was going wrong within the youth; decadence, promiscuity... you name it. For some reason, Madonna was the cause of it all. But for a brief time, back in 1983, Madonna was just a pop singer, delivering her modern disco beats and vitality to the pop world. Still, even in such early days, she was sure of what she wanted to achieve, and what she swore would be around the corner.

"I now know what I want on my next record," Madonna told the NME at the back end of 83. "The producer won't be so slick. I want a sound that's mine. There will be a more crossover approach to it this time. Maybe I should work with a British producer."

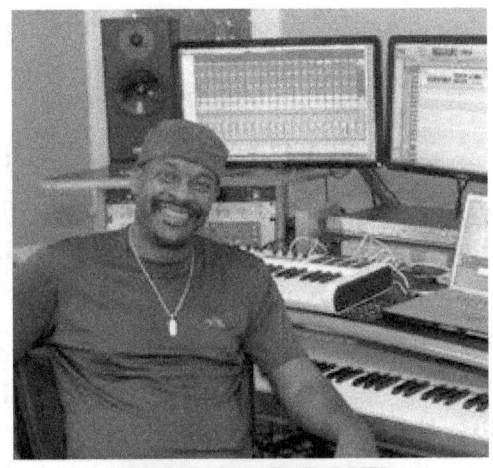

DEAN GANT

ON WORKING WITH MADONNA

Dean Gant played synthesizer and piano on the first Madonna album. Here, he recalls his memories of working the young and ambitious Queen in waiting...

Do you remember first hearing about Madonna?

In 1982 when Reggie Lucas called me about doing a new project on "this singer" who had a dance tune that was breaking out in NY.

How did you first meet her? What was she like?

First time was in the recording studio, Sigma Sound. She was very cool and friendly, we hit it off right away.

What are your memories of recording on the first album? What did your job on that record entail?

Kind of a tricky question... I was Reggie Lucas's go-to keyboardist, arranger, synth guy etc. I was also producing stuff on my own, but Mtume/Lucas were a hot team at the time. So I basically took all the songs and arranged them from demos that Madonna had. My input on some was greater than arranging; for instance Lucky Star, I basically wrote most of the music, (uncredited or paid), but the bridge I totally created and the chord changes. Madonna had the hook line vocal and a 3 note bass line idea.

Did Madonna seem in control and know what she wanted in the studio?

She definitely had her own ideas about what she wanted, but a lot of things weren't expressed until after we finished and she basically had a disagreement with Reggie. That's when she brought in Jelly Bean, who changed some of the tracks around, but kept most of the major stuff we did.

Did you enjoy playing on the tracks? Which was the most fun to do?

Yes it was a very enjoyable project, Madonna was a lot of fun, we hung out at different times. Borderline was cool and interesting in that the wonderful bassist Anthony Jackson and I played the bass part simultaneously live in the control room of the studio. Most people don't know that it is both a synth bass and electric bass. Another fun

74

song was I Know It, for which I came up with a neo-classical synth string intro.

How did you figure out your parts? Did Madonna say what she wanted at all?

I created all of my parts, Madonna never really suggested anything, she like pretty much everything I came up with. We were pretty much in sync.

Do any memories stick out from the recordings?

Yeah, quite a few... Madonna and a male dancer who was around quite a bit, dancing in the studio, really going wild when I put the bass part on Lucky Star; also a girl I was dating who was a model was hanging out and her and Madonna hit it off quite well. Also I went to support her at a live show she had at a club called the Red Parrot, and she was very appreciative of me coming out, as no one else who was working on the project came out to hear her.

How do you look back on the era and working with Madonna?

It was a fun time, a very creative time. We did not have any template for what we did with her. We just created a sound that was dance, R&B, pop and synth heavy, which was my specialty. Again Madonna was great to work with, one of the most fun projects I have ever done. There was no doubt that it was going to be successful, we just didn't know it was going to blow up like it did.

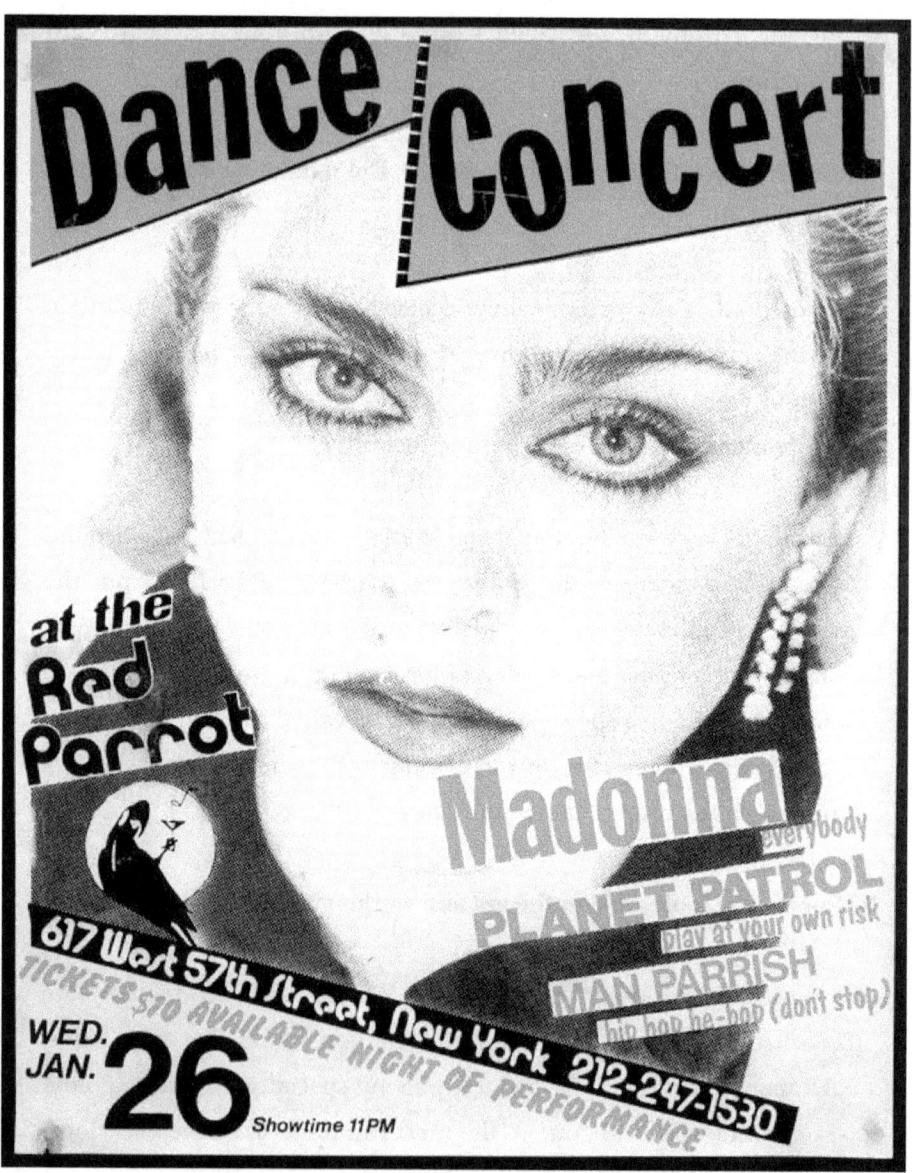

Dance/Concert

at the
Red
Parrot

Madonna
everybody

PLANET PATROL
play at your own risk

MAN PARRISH
hip hop be-bop (don't stop)

617 West 57th Street, New York 212-247-1530

TICKETS $10 AVAILABLE NIGHT OF PERFORMANCE

WED. JAN. 26
Showtime 11PM

76

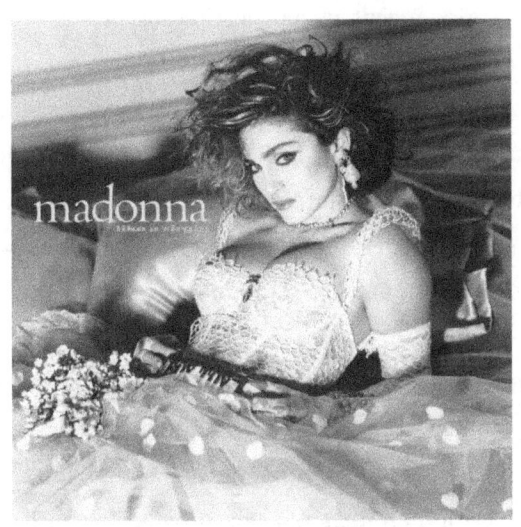

<u>LIKE A VIRGIN</u>
THE MATERIAL GIRL GETS HER CROWN

"My work, my dedication—the stubbornness for getting Madonna released—had paid off. Now it was time to solidify my future."

For many, though the first album has some killer tunes and its own set of charms, Madonna's true arrival came with the release of the Like A Virgin album. Much more worked out, calculate and polished, it is undoubtedly a great album, but in my view only equals the power and vitality of her debut. Her first album was more raw, more wide eyed and naive. Sure there was the hope of success and stardom in there, and at times it jumped out of the songs in desperation. But with Like A Virgin, it was clear that Madonna was a star and was going to be an even bigger one thanks to the sharp, punctuated, expertly crafted and highly polished follow up. Even looking at the cover, you know the album has a sense of much deserved self importance. It looks like a statement, and that is because it truly is. It's Madonna's statement though, despite the well known help she had during its creation; and that statement seems to say, quite clearly, "I'm here!"

It's been over emphasised and written to death, but Like A Virgin also marked the first time Madonna changed her image and look (and though fewer people mention it, her sound too), as if settling into a character for her next play or movie., In truth, that is what Madonna does; she is an actor in the fullest sense, and pulls another face, approach, and persona from her endless wardrobe of identities to keep it fresh for the listener, the viewer, and most importantly, herself. There is nothing weird about her reinventions, as some have suggested. After all, she is just being creative, artistic, playing with her own image and the collective image of women all over the world. There is no end to who she can be in her music. She is selling herself, nothing evil or worthy of the kind of criticism she attracts.

In a 2009 interview, Rolling Stone mentioned that there was a massive shift between the first and second albums, not only in Madonna's image, but also the songs and the music as a whole. She was straight forward in her reply. "I guess the music I started to write had more of a seductive quality," she replied, "and I unconsciously morphed into that. It also had to do with the fact that I was doing more photo shoots. I was being styled and dressed. Before that, I was doing everything myself. I had no makeup artist, I was taking my dance tights and tying them around my head and throwing a few rosaries around my neck. After that, it was [photographer] Steven Meisel, and fashion people putting me in corsets. I think people put a lot of emphasis on the whole reinvention of my image, and it's always been a lot less calculated than people think. It's just evolution and what I'm interested in, the books I read or movies or clothes that I see. Just call me Zelig. Wasn't that the Woody Allen movie where he took on the personality of whoever he's talking to? I think it's boring to stay the same. A girl likes to change her look."

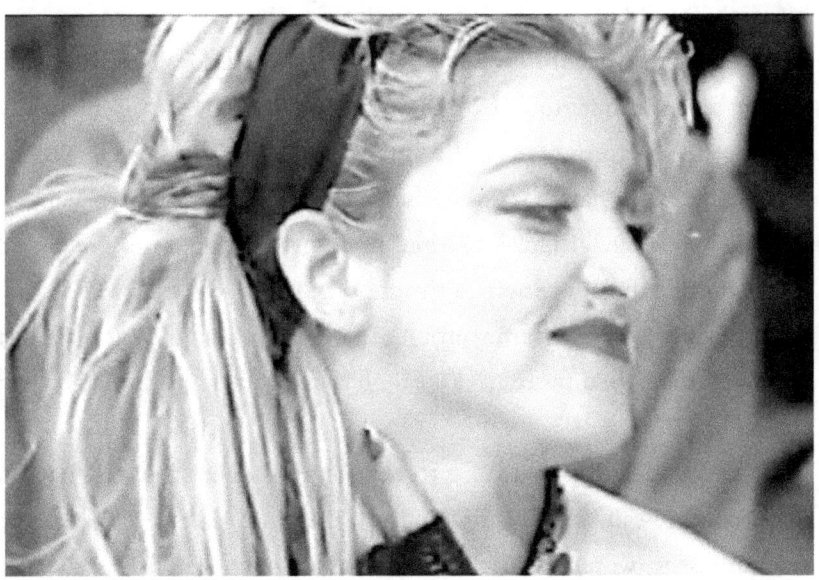

If you are merely looking at the album as a collection of images adopted by one individual, then you could ask yourself what album *isn't* a collection of adopted characteristics when we are discussing any LP of various moods? Like A Virgin as a group of songs is not like some drastically varying Lon Chaney type gallery of faces. It is in fact a straight forward pop record, and only on a couple of songs does Madonna adopt an ironic edge, twisting the songs into directions we might have not expected. Had she been a man, nobody would have cared what persona or viewpoint she took on for any given song. But as she was a young female in her mid twenties with a lot to prove to a chauvinistic industry, it took a little more getting used to - and that's an understatement if there ever was one.

Ever ambitious, Madonna had wanted to be the sole or main producer on her second album, but Warner Brothers did not feel she could hold an album on her own just yet. "Warner Bros. Records is a hierarchy of old men and it's a chauvinist environment to be working in because I'm treated like this sexy little girl," Madonna bravely said at the time. "I had to prove them wrong, which meant not only proving myself to my fans but to my record company as well. That is something that happens when you're a girl. It wouldn't happen to Prince or Michael Jackson. I had to do everything on my own and it was hard trying to convince people that I was worth a record deal. After that, I had the same problem trying to convince the record company that I had more to offer than a one-shot singer. I had to win this fight."

Seeing as Madonna did have to choose a producer to assist her on her second LP, she opted for Chic front man and whizz producer Nile Rodgers, who would lend the album a lot of its vitality, funk and grooviness. It was to be a drastic shift from her poppy, bubbly, dance debut, but it was a shift which was very welcome, and much needed at the time. The album was put down at Power Station Studio in New York City, with former Chic band mates backing him up throughout, among other session players. "I am always amazed by Madonna's incredible judgement when it comes to making pop records," Rodgers later said. "I've never seen anyone do it better, and that's the truth. When we did that album, it was the perfect union, and I knew it from the first day in the studio. The thing between us, man, it was sexual, it was passionate, it was creativity... it was pop."

There is no denying that Like A Virgin is a truly great pop record, and each and every time I listen to it (which is a lot over the years) it never seems to lose any of its punch, its magic, or its energy. An album of moods (to cite a cliché), it is also a show case for Madonna the singer, the interpreter, the pop star, the actress, the icon and the temptress. She gets to try on a lot of hats throughout, and they all fit perfectly.

Few records have ever opened better than this one did, with the undeniable excitement of Material Girl. The music has an energy and bounce which makes it the perfect album opener, all crunchy drums, sharp synths and inventive melodic touches in the mix. Again though, it's that voice which seals the deal, with Madonna at her squeakiest and most poppy. The song was actually not written by Madonna at all, but a co-write between Peter Brown and Robert Rans. Featuring an iconic vocal performance (and an almost equally iconic refrain by Frank Simms), the song became a reluctant anthem, a theme tune for Madonna's career. The "material girl" cliché had begun, and for decades it was seen as Madonna's signature song, and became a regular pun in articles and tabloid coverage thereafter. The song is undoubtedly good, but the irony and indeed the message (or what it meant to Madonna as its singer) have been lost over the years; and indeed, were lost as soon as the song was released.

Some have argued that irony and pop do not mix, but they are wrong, it all just depends on who is listening and what they are choosing to hear in the song. I see Material Girl as one of hooks that Madonna used to get herself imbedded into popular culture. She knew the Marilyn Monroe tribute video would be an instant classic, and that it would make people talk. That it was released slap bang in the middle of the 1980s, the era of Thatcher, Reagan, greed, power, big shoulder pads, even bigger hair and low values, heightened its impact. Clearly, the fact that Madonna thought people would clearly see the irony illustrates how much faith she had in pop buyers, and how she saw pop as a true outlet, within which you could say whatever you felt like saying. Thirty odd years later, pop seems even less like a medium in which you can vent rage, use sharp irony and make a point, but in the mid 1980s, Madonna was one of the few people who thought it could be useful as a mirror of society, reflecting our flaws and shining them, warts and all, right back at us. She was perhaps a little too ahead of her time, and indeed any time by the look of things.

"I can't completely disdain the song and the video," Madonna later said, "because they certainly were important to my career. But talk about the media hanging on a phrase and misinterpreting the damn thing as well. I didn't write that song, you know, and the video was about how the girl rejected diamonds and money. But God forbid irony should be understood. So when I'm ninety, I'll still be the Material Girl. I guess it's not so bad. Lana Turner was the Sweater Girl until the day she died."

Even more recently, she was still annoyed by the song. Speaking to Howard Stern, she said, "The song that irritated me the most about being associated with me is Material Girl. It was an ironic song because I'm certainly not a materialistic person."

Though the song is classic pop, legendary music today, one can understand Madonna's negative views towards it. Being associated with a song you did not even write, let alone properly believe in, is certainly hell on earth for an ambitious, addictive creator like Madonna. But overlooking this, one can enjoy Material Girl for the anthem it is... with irony and all.

One song which Madonna did help write, and certainly one she should be proud of, is the beautiful Angel. With its rich musical arrangement (full keyboards, imaginative melodies, bubbling synth lines) and sad, slightly melancholic vocal, Madonna sends the song into magical territory. She sings of a man who must be some kind of angel, a being who is almost holy, separate from the crowds he stands out from. This man is a saviour, arriving out of nowhere to whisk her away and take her to some dream land, a perfect love in a perfect world. To Madonna it was about a girl "in depression over something. An angel appeared and healed her soul, making her fall madly in love with Him. It's something that I felt when I was young. I thought it would make for an interesting story if I wrote that experience as a song on my record."

In the midst of the album, it is far and away one of the strongest cuts here (perhaps my favourite if I am pushed to come up with one) and was also a stand alone hit single in its own right. Coming after the contrived ironies of Material Girl, Angel seems more straight forward, more honest. Musically it has a strong and sturdy punch to it, a back drop which juxtaposes beautifully with Madonna's rich vocal performance. Real pop gold.

The title track is, once again, beyond pop legend, but it's another song which should not be taken as an honest narrative song or a Madonna anthem from her own voice and outlook. Written by Tom Kelly and Billy Steinberg, it's another non-Madonna penned song which she does not hold entirely dear. If it's down to her stern ambition that she should not adopt someone else's song as one of her chosen anthems, or more down to the fact that the song says very little about her view of the world, it's one which she revisits from time to time as an ironic curiosity. Though the song has a passionate drive, great music and a hooky chorus (the verses aren't too shabby either), it is not key in understanding the Madonna sphere. Provocative yes, and certainly playful, the song introduces the idea of a newly gained love making someone feel "shiny and new", as if they are experiencing love, passion and intimacy for the first time.

As expressed in a brilliant Spin interview upon the album's release, Madonna explained her own definition of virginity, and it was not as literal as some critics might have thought. "I wouldn't like to sleep with a guy who was a virgin. I'd have to teach him stuff and I don't have the patience. I'd rather deal with experience. When I say virgin, like in my song, I'm not thinking about sexual virgin. I mean newness. Even after I made love for the first time, I still felt like I was a virgin. I didn't lose my virginity until I knew what I was doing."

"I mean, I was surprised with how people reacted to Like A Virgin," Madonna told Rolling Stone at the time, "because when I did the song, to me, I was singing about how something made me feel a certain way – brand new and fresh – and everyone else interpreted it as I don't want to be a virgin anymore. F*ck my brains out! That's not what I sang at all." For the second of many times, they had taken

Madonna's lyrics the completely wrong way, forming their own opinions of what she really meant and labeling her however they chose to.

If we are focusing on the impact and sonic joys of the said record though, few could realistically raise issues with it. Catchy as hell, wonderfully produced and cheeky to boot, it's one of the most iconic pop songs of the 1980s, and though we may all have our favourite Madonna songs (however deep they are in an album's play list), this is undoubtedly one of her best known and most loved songs.

The real problem with Madonna's music, or at least how the public and music press judged it, was that they chose to focus more on "her" and her image, her sexiness, her sassiness and her viewpoints, as opposed to the songs, the sound and her singing voice. It seems odd when perusing interviews of the day in the archives that few people seem to care about the music. Of course, Madonna's image and look was and is vital to pop history (and cultural history too), but surely the music is what made her known. Yet still, even today, there are few books devoted to exploring the dichotomies of her music and lyrics, not to mention the sound, the feel and the importance of the arrangements.

That said, and with that in mind, Madonna is starting to really have an idea of who and what she is on the Like A Virgin album; and though many believe her voice only really improved when she got the training and did Evita in the 1990s, and that her songs only gained depth in the later part of the 1980s on Like A Prayer, Like A Virgin shows that her voice was already improving, and that her songs had a depth to them, a sadness, a weight and a sense of slight melancholia - all beneath the highly charged pop surface of course.

When asked by one magazine if all her songs were about love, Madonna said no, stating that Over and Over, the album's fourth track, was about ambition. With a smoother, calmer, cooler vocal effort (much deeper too, with more control on the melodies), the song coasts by on its simple but appealing arrangement. Again, Madonna's voice comes out front. Here she displays her strength, exposing her drive, her willingness to get up again after falling, trying and trying until she succeeds. She is the powerful new woman of the 1980s, singing with defiance and self belief.

Madonna shows her true range on track five with her spellbinding, heart breaking and utterly powerful take on the Miles Gregory classic Love Don't Live Here Anymore. An inspired choice for a cover, it was a brave move to cut such a well known, highly regarded song on her second studio record, while still trying to prove herself as her own entity. But she gives the song a new identity, her vocals soaring, expressive and deeply affecting. It is probably her first truly great vocal effort, in every way a "performance" akin to an actor taking on someone else's skin. She is Madonna the balladeer, the power house wailer, shuffled in there amidst the speedier, more poppy material. Musically too, Rodgers has excelled; it's expansive, dramatic, cinematic almost, but not over cooked. Madonna's voice, as it should be, remains centre stage and the main focal point. Few critics picked it out at the time as a highlight (in fact, some said it was a low point of the record) but today it remains something of a hidden gem. It was later included on her ballads compilation, the excellent Something to Remember.

Though it was not included on the original edition, Into the Groove showed up on the 1985 re-release of the album. Taken from her hit movie Desperately Seeking Susan, the song is one of Madonna's most iconic. Written by her and Stephen Bray, it feels very much like a Madonna cut, and does not have the jokey, almost cartoon like silliness of Like A Virgin and Material Girl. The song could have come off her debut LP, in that the message seems to be "dance and forget". She is inviting the lucky guy on to the dance floor of life to

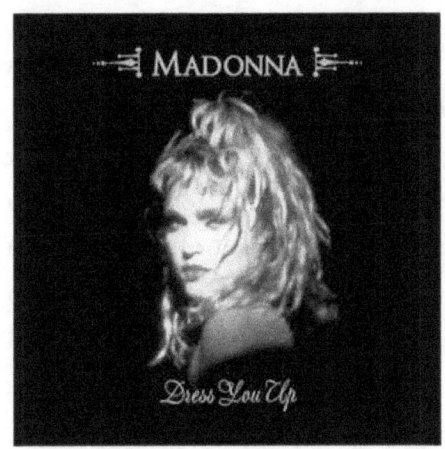

live out his fantasies with her. Musically, the song remains vital sounding and exciting, its full bass line driving it along like an engine that refuses to stop. One of her purest songs, it remains undeniably solid.

"When I was writing it, I was sitting in a fourth-floor walk-up on Avenue-B," she told Time Magazine, "and there was this gorgeous Puerto Rican boy sitting across me that I wanted to go out on a date with, and I just wanted to get the song over with. I ultimately did go out with him and the song was finished just before my last date with him, which I'm kinda happy that it did not continue... The dance floor was quite a magical place for me. I started off wanting to be a dancer, so that had a lot to do with the song. The freedom that I always feel when I'm dancing, that feeling of inhabiting your body, letting yourself go, expressing yourself through music. I always thought of it as a magical place – even if you're not taking ecstasy. Hence that came to me as the primary inspiration for Into the Groove."

Dress You Up was another one released as single (another hit too), but as Madonna did not write it, I am not sure how close to her heart the song really is. With a solid drum beat, neat guitar and keyboard interplay, and an immovable bass line, it's musically very striking. Again though, Madonna's voice sticks out and gets right to the heart of things. She's in love again, playing the part of the lusty, impassioned woman perfectly. It's not her song, but it is definitely her performance, and she owns it from the first line to the last. It has an irresistible chorus too, easily one of the best from this era.

Shoo Bee Doo is another song which may seem underwhelming at first, but actually reveals layers of the future Madonna, the more developed woman and artist. Tenderly she sings of confusion over a haunting piano line in a wonderful intro, which soon kicks into action 40 seconds in. With punchy drums, sweet keyboards and another driven synth bass line, Madonna's voice is clear in the mix. She sounds exposed and vulnerable. The lyrics are sad but beautiful, and bring to mind later Madonna gems (this is the one track on the record where she has sole writing credit, it seems fitting to add), especially in the emotional, diving delivery. There is a power to her voice and her control of it which separates it from other songs on the record, and it feels a cut above the rest. This is not something I have always felt though. In my younger years, I saw it as filler, lesser material which suffered as a result of being put side by side with immortal anthems. Now though, in my thirties, the song reveals a complexity, a hurt and depth that transcends the better known material hands down, and is actually more accomplished. This is mature song writing, showing that at the mere age of 26, Madonna was already a serious song writer capable of reaching the soul.

Wonderfully structured, beautifully sung and painfully underrated, it remains a hidden gem I keep returning to more and more as the years go by.

The last two songs are probably the lesser ones on an album crammed full of rich gold, but they are still enjoyable slices of vintage Madonna. Pretender is hooky and good fun, another song of obsessive love, played and produced tightly. Madonna's vocals are as strong as they are on the rest of the record, and this co write with Bray remains solid. Stay is the album's closer, and it sounds off the album nicely. Though minor, it has a great bounce to it (the drums are very good here) and Madonna sounds, if less emotional and frantic, more assured, relaxed and at ease, finishing off her star record like a true pro.

Though a lot of the press were seeing her music as so-so, a fad about to pass and lacking in substance, others pounced on her individuality. Washington Post wrote a great article about her new album in 1984. They noted her humour, her sense of irony, and more importantly, the fact she could adapt to each song, and morph her persona to fit varying moods and shades. "Her voice isn't powerful," they wrote, "but it is remarkably expressive, allowing her to convey a depth of personality that goes well beyond the specifics of her material. On the title song of her new album, Like a Virgin (Sire 25157-1), she neatly skips past the lyrics' simple metaphor of being reborn through true love and, with a nudge and a wink, transforms it into a delicious bit of naughtiness. Madonna presents a couple of variations on this approach, ranging from the breathless physicality of Dress You Up to the almost maternal devotion of Shoo-Bee Doo, and what stands out most in each is the singer's ability to put across the credible personality. It's not quite the same thing as assuming a new role for every number, because there is a certain constancy to her delivery that suggests there's a bit of Madonna in all her poses. While that's flattering enough in a song like Over And Over, an upbeat celebration of determination, it's somewhat less so in Material Girl, which at one point quips that 'The boy with the cold hard cash/ Is always Mr. Right.' Yet the fact that Madonna appreciates the truth in the joke makes her performance all the more delightful. Madonna's singing is always the central attraction on the album, but an equal amount of credit is due producer Nile Rodgers, who delivers backing tracks that are both insistently propulsive and perfectly suited to Madonna's delivery."

Indeed, listening again, perhaps in light of more recent tours and albums, and one can see that even album number two into her career, she knew what she was doing, and had a grasp of moods, styles and approaches, more so than any of her contemporaries. Seeing as it was released so long ago now, one can put aside the sweeping Madonna craze, the fame, the head spinning heady days she experienced in 84 and 85, and most importantly over look the massive sales, and see that this album, quite clearly, stands alone and more than stands the test of time, musically, lyrically and as a whole experience. Many records of the day have dated, and their sagginess has been as a result of the simple passage of time and what has come since. Like A Virgin, though, is definitely not one of these albums. It may sum up the mid 1980s as much as Thriller and Back to the Future, but it also exists outside that time frame, and also outside of Madonna's discography, as well as being an integral part of her musical development. A classic album, with killer song after killer song, all produced with precision and delivered with emotion, gusto and passion. Madonna was a true star, and even without her iconic image in your face on the posters, album covers and music videos, Like A Virgin is a great album - quite simply, a classic.

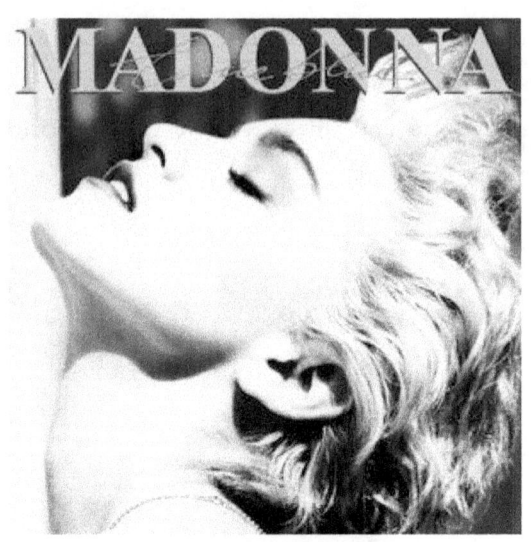

TRUE BLUE
THE MEGA SELLER RE-EXAMINED

As much as her doubters might have liked her to disappear as quickly from view as she had emerged into the spotlight, they must have been sorely disappointed when she came back to the charts in 1986 with what many saw as her best album yet. True Blue was a consistently strong record by anyone's standards, and turned out to be a huge seller, shifting an inconceivable amount, and catapulting Madonna into a level of fame only a handful of people have ever known. An icon had arrived, and she wasn't going anywhere.

"True Blue was really a labour of love, and I'm very proud of it," Madonna told Seventeen Magazine back in 1986. In the interview she also told the press who the album was made for - her beau, actor Sean Penn. "I'd never heard the expression 'true blue' until I met

Sean, who uses it all the time. The album is dedicated to him. It's a special album, because it says exactly what I wanted it to say. I wrote almost all the lyrics and felt the freedom to do whatever I wanted in the studio. The record is about someone who is growing up, who wants to be strong and go after what she wants. But there is also more sadness in the songs on this record than on my first two albums. Live to Tell is a very sad song that I wrote for Sean's movie At Close Range. It's about being very young and having to grow up quickly because you've seen certain things that force you to be a grown-up ahead of your time."

The first album had been a straight forward, head-first dive into dance and disco, the joys of life on the dance floor; Like A Virgin had been an ironic slice of pop art, containing a few pensive moments but basically coming across as light hearted fun. True Blue, as Madonna stated in her interview for Seventeen, certainly did have more of a sad edge, though there was still plenty of danceable pop and feel good beats to please the millions she had won over with her previous two records. That said, the melancholia I am such a fan of (Madonna is at her best when melancholic in my view, preferably to a sad and beautiful melody) was creeping in and lending her work much more depth, human frailty and an edge that transcended what her harshest critics had to say about her.

True Blue did for music in the mid 1980s what the likes of Revolver and Sgt. Pepper did in the 1960s. Introducing - and indeed mixing - pop, rock and classical elements to a young audience (and judging by the huge sales, it certainly won her a few older fans too), the album has an air of grace and class about it, is wonderfully put together and executed, with top class production from Madonna, Patrick Leonard and Stephen Bray.

Papa Don't Preach is a superb opener, and as far as first-songs on Madonna's albums go, it's probably the best of the 1980s. The debut had begun in style with Lucky Star, Like A Virgin had been instantly punchy and fun with Material Girl, and Like A Prayer would later start with one of her most iconic songs, the album's title track. But True Blue being kick started by Papa Don't Preach and its imposing classical introduction is hard to beat, and will forever remain so for future artists.

It starts with those regal orchestral/keyboard chords, as if signalling the arrival of royalty - and in this case, it truly is. With a chunky bass line leading the rhythm alongside a solid drum beat, the song is also filled out with keyboards, subtle in the mix, which add melodies and nice touches here and there. Then Madonna's voice comes in, warm and familiar by now (third album in and all), singing with all her heart. Moralistic and serious in tone, the compelling condensed masterpiece tells the tale of a young girl who is pregnant to her new love, and begs for her dad's support. Written by Brian Elliot and plucked by Bray and Leonard, Madonna put in a few touches lyric wise, but the song is mostly Elliott's, which makes it stand out from the other tracks on True Blue, otherwise penned by Madonna and her co-writers.

Even though Papa Don't Preach was not her own personal song, much like earlier anthems such as Material Girl and Like A Virgin, Madonna invested so much emotion into it that you would swear it was autobiographical. You can hear her pain, her confusion and her desperation when pleading with her father. When she later told one interviewer that her performances in song and video were "like what De Niro does", changing her voice and approach as an actor might, her explanation made more sense than those who still accuse her of being a social vampire, a morphing opportunist who shifts shapes to fit the song or trend in question. In Papa Don't Preach, one must only watch the video and take in her emotion during the song to realise this is a performance through and through, just as complex, well observed and brilliantly executed as one of our greatest actors fleshing out a role. The only difference is, they get 90 minutes plus to get it across; Madonna, in the case of Papa Don't Preach and other classics from this time, only gets 5 minutes. Still, this condensed performance is multi faceted and deeply believable, despite her limited time. It is a testament to her talent that she could get to the core of the character so speedily.

On the subject of the song itself, Madonna was very open, especially in her frank one-on-one with Seventeen Magazine. "People will take the song wrong and assume that I'm telling every young girl to go out and get pregnant. I'll admit that when I first heard it, I thought, 'Oh, please — I'm going to keep my baby?' It seemed silly. But the more I thought about it, the more I realized it was about a girl who is making a decision in her life. She has a really close relationship with her father and wants to maintain it. To me, the song is positive, because she wants to make it work. One writer said recently that I liked to 'wade into the fire.' I hadn't thought about it until I read those words, but I think it's true. I don't like things to be black-and-white."

In a chat with Interview Magazine in 1986, Madonna went on further, stating "Papa Don't Preach is a message song that everyone is going to take the wrong way. Immediately they're going to say I am advising every young girl to go out and get pregnant. When I first heard the song, I thought it was silly. But then I thought, wait a minute, this song is really about a girl who is making a decision in her life. She has a very close relationship with her father and wants to maintain that closeness. To me it's a celebration of life. It says, 'I love you, father, and I love this man and this child that is growing inside me.' Of course, who knows how it will end? But at least it starts off positive."

To Rolling Stone in 2009, she was more defiant, seeing the song as a feminist theme tune. "The song just fit right in with my own personal zeitgeist of standing up to male authorities, whether it's the pope, or the Catholic Church or my father and his conservative, patriarchal ways... For Papa Don't Preach there were so many opinions – that's why I thought it was so great. Is she for 'schma-smortion', as they say in Knocked Up? Is she against abortion?"

Madonna refused to stand up and voice her opinion on abortion when the song raised issues within rights groups. She cited the track as having a very important message, it just happened to be one she did not want to express her true views on - and perhaps wisely so. In one statement, her press agent Liz Rosenberg told the New York Times, "She's singing a song, not taking a stand. Her philosophy is people can think what they want to think." After all, an artist's role is to point out and question, to raise issues and air them out for the receptor to react to. The artist does not tell the listener what to think and how to feel. Madonna is no exception.

Others were enraged by her decision to sing about teenage pregnancy but not talk about it. Alfred Moran, head of Planned

Parenthood in New York during the mid 1980s, was quoted as saying "The message is that getting pregnant is cool and having the baby is the right thing and a good thing and don't listen to your parents, the school, anybody who tells you otherwise - don't preach to me, Papa. The reality is that what Madonna is suggesting to teen-agers is a path to permanent poverty. Everybody I've talked to believes she has more impact on young teenagers than any other single entertainer since the Beatles. That's what makes this particular song so destructive."

But one can look at this from another perspective. If an actress played a pregnant woman in a movie, would she too be called upon to make her views known, or would it be accepted as being merely a film role? Why then, should Madonna be questioned and harassed, all because she is operating in the field of pop music, a medium many still believe is not the place for serious issues to be explored. Novels and plays are fine, but pop songs? Get out of here.

Though she did not fully write it, Papa Don't Preach was proof that Madonna was much more than a pop princess singing about dancing and letting loose, and nothing else. Social issues were not out of her zone now, and in choosing to approach this serious song and give it dramatic gravitas, she shifted herself (and pop too) up a few gears. This was not merely bubble gum pop, this was art, music which spoke directly to the listener, was well played and produced at the same time as being challenging and, perhaps for the first time in Madonna's career, rather controversial. There was plenty more to come of course.

Open Your Heart is the follow up track, a danceable hit in every respect which from the first second is much more innocent, fun and straight forward. Madonna co-wrote it with Gardner Cole and Peter

Rafelson (the pair had originally written it as Follow Your Heart, but Madonna revamped it and rewrote the lyrics), and though not harboring the depth and raw emotion of Papa Don't Preach, it is classic Madonna and was an instant favourite among fans upon release of the album, and when the song became a stand alone hit single in November of 1986. With its bouncing synths, chiming keyboards, funky guitars and heavy drums, it could have been lifted from her previous album, stylistically being very much like Like A Virgin in its sound. However, the feel is different, too. For one, Madonna's voice is more controlled than it had been on much of her first two albums; deeper too, harboring none of the squeakiness of those early, heady disco hits. There is true sincerity to her vocals here, a warmth and a genuine feeling that she is into the role one hundred percent. Madonna was in love with Penn by now, and though she played roles which varied on each number, here she sounds deeply immersed. Was the emotion so present on this song (just listen to how she howls out the chorus, shiver inducing stuff) dug up from her genuine love for Sean Penn? Was this actress now method acting? When Madonna tells the boy to open his heart, she demands so with so much power that no one would dare to defy her.

White Heat begins with a voice sample of the great and then newly late film legend James Cagney, taken from his classic gangster picture... yep, White Heat. Many cite the track as album filler, but I feel it's a gem in its own right. Three tracks in and Madonna is ensuring True Blue has a warm and inviting sound, and while White Heat rocks a little more than the first two numbers, it is just as accessible as Open Your Heart. Again, she is asking (or demanding) the man taker her seriously and see that her love is real. This time, however, it's dangerous. It leads into what for me remains the strongest and most arresting song on the album, the towering Live to Tell. One of Madonna's most powerful moments, it was her first truly deep, introspective and heavily melancholic song up to that point in time.

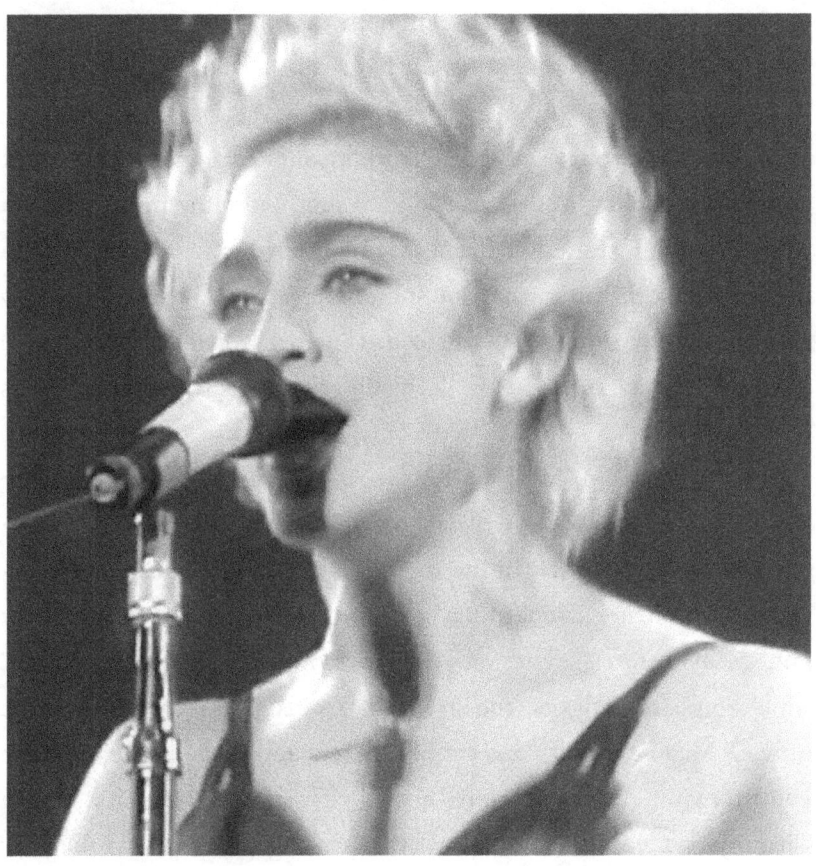

Live to Tell originated as an instrumental sent to Paramount for inclusion in a film called Fire With Fire, but they turned it down. Patrick Leonard, disappointed but not beaten, took the demo to Madonna and asked her to write some lyrics. She did so, and on top of that altered it melodically and made it her own. Though it was also used for the soundtrack of the James Foley classic At Close Range (starring Penn and Christopher Walken), Live to Tell made its way on to True Blue and if truth be told, lifted the record up a scale with its depth and heavyweight gravitas. Madonna's voice, over the delicately produced and structured backing track, is real, very much a "performance" (I keep coming back to this word, but that is what these songs are for Madonna) in as much as she loses herself in the narrative of the song. Her voice had not sounded so pure and honest before. The backing vocals, mixed very subtly into the mix, are also a wonder, and illustrate her strength within her range. Perhaps it is in the pairing with the music, but something about Live to Tell really gets to me every time I listen to it. Cinematic, deeply moving and flawless, it remains Madonna perfection and one of the finest songs from the 1980s.

Many have cited Live to Tell as a landmark moment in her development, with Mojo writing in 2015 that it was something of a "creative breakthrough." In the interview, for the magazine Madonna says that co writer Leonard has a dark side to him ("Yeah that's very fair," is his retort) but it was her lyrics, mysterious and enigmatic, which gave the song its true strength. "It was kind of inspired by the movie," Madonna said, "and family secrets and the things that make you who you are, but you don't necessarily want to share. Mix that in with my own childhood and my own growing up and all of that. My real experiences get mixed in with things that I imagine."

She also spoke of the song in her 2009 Rolling Stone interview, singling it out when speaking about the way songs almost pass through her, rather than coming out from an intense thought process. "Sometimes when I'm writing songs, I'm just channelling," she said. "I could say that Live To Tell was about my childhood, my relationship with my parents, my father and my stepmother. But maybe not. It could be about something in an F. Scott Fitzgerald novel or a story that I heard once. It's true, but it's not necessarily autobiographical."

Madonna's explanation makes sense. While people have said she writes in a stream of consciousness sort of way, channelling makes much more sense. As in Oh Father and other ballads, Madonna mixes fiction with reality. In the case of Oh Father, we all know her father was not abusive in real life, but she mixes her own past with drama to create a more "real" and rounded song which feels truer to the listener, and indeed to Madonna herself., She may just have adopted the same technique for Live to Tell, for though it is very dramatic and filmic, it also feels as if it came from the pit of her stomach, the depths of her subconscious. It makes sense that she revived it for her 2006 Confessions tour, and chose to combine the song with some pretty graphic religious imagery (she was singing it on the cross as a tribute to Jesus Christ himself). Religion and sex, Madonna's two great obsessions, repeatedly overlap in the singer's career; an example of the duality of her creative outlook. In this case, Live to Tell proved to be a lasting and meaningful song for her, adapting itself into mutated forms twenty years on from its creation.

Where's the Party? is much lighter, a fairly standard Madonna dance track that defines "fun" in the best possible sense. She once said she wrote the song to remind herself that, 'hey, this is meant to be fun,' and that shines through the glowing arrangement and her vital

101

vocal performance. Stylistically similar to White Heat, it has a bounce and drive to it which makes it infectious, and by putting this and White Heat at either side of Live to Tell, Madonna ensured the album did not get too heavy, even though that would not have been a bad thing at all. But Madonna took Where's the Party? as an opportunity to lighten herself up, forget the stress of fame, the quick pace of life, the fact she was moving too fast, and let her hair down for once. She had worked and slaved for this fame (though she never expected the fame to be quite so big, as she said in one interview), but now it was time for a breather. I hope Madonna enjoyed this "break", because let's face it, she wasn't going to take many more.

True Blue, the title track, is another joyous little detour, this one a tribute to the doo-wopping girl groups of the 50s and 60s. In three time, the familiar chord pattern makes way for a sweet Madonna vocal and melody, surely one of the girliest and more delicate moments on the record. Amazingly, Madonna revived the song in 2015 nearly thirty years later for her Rebel Heart tour, playing the song on the ukulele, making the stadiums cry collectively and taking the track to a whole new level. Its feel is one of pure love, and Bray says it was inspired by her adoration for Penn. Years later, Madonna herself said it was a song about true love in the truest sense, but claimed to not know what she was singing about specifically.

La Isla Bonita is certainly one of the most accomplished songs on the record, and has not aged one bit (interestingly, Madonna revived this one on her Rebel Heart tour too). Latin in flavour, this exotic pop gem is perfectly structured, neatly produced and marvelously sung by Madonna, who takes you straight out to the land of sunshine, dancing and good times.

Madonna worked on the song with Leonard and songwriter Bruce Gaitsch, who had initially sent the tune to Michael Jackson for his Bad album, but saw it turned down. In a thrilling moment, given that the song has been a favourite of mine for decades, I spoke with Bruce Gaitsch a few years ago all about the writing of that Madonna classic. "My pal Patrick Leonard was working with her," Bruce told me. "He and I had a studio and we recorded some demos and co-wrote a song for her." Does he recall his first meeting with Madonna? "Yes I do, it was at Leeds Rehearsal Facility in LA. Patrick, Jonathan Moffit, David Williams and I were trying to see if she liked playing with a live band. She had never done it before. Bill Meyers and a Bill Lamphier were the rest of the band. We rehearsed for two days and she enjoyed herself. Toto was in the next room and they kept walking by asking which one of us was Madonna. Until she arrived, then the door was locked."

Of the actual writing process, he recalled "Patrick and I wrote the music and sent it to her in China where she was working with Sean Penn on a movie (Shanghai Surprise). I never was in a room with her until we recorded it. Madonna was the easiest person to work with that I have ever worked with. She never second guessed herself, she heard it right once and said 'That's it. Time is money and it's my fucking money!' I was and am still thrilled. I am the luckiest man in the world. Madonna is a throwback to the days when you had to be able to sing, dance, act and write to be a star. She does it all with no apparent effort... she is my hero."

Madonna made the song a loving tribute to the "beauty and mystery of Latin American people", and she took the opportunity to adopt the Latin rhythm and outlook, another character she perfected for the sublime four minutes of this immortal gem.

As with Like A Virgin, True Blue ends with what I see as the two lesser songs on the record, though they are still wonderful additions to the multi faceted prism of the LP as a whole. Jimmy Jimmy is fluffy and light, with a catchy refrain of the title after each verse line. Much lighter and sillier than much of Madonna's other output from this era, it still has an air of magic about it, wonderfully produced as it is. Love Makes the World Go Round is a worthy closer, very 80s in its rich production and again defining the word fun effortlessly. Madonna gives a tremendous vocal effort here, both warm and soulful, firing high and low on the range of her abilities. Musically quirky, it has a great rhythm to it, and also a killer chorus, ending the album in a light hearted, optimistic view. Again, Madonna is loved up, and she fades us out with genuine glee.

While True Blue sold almost four times as much as Like A Virgin, this does not mean it is necessarily a better album, at least not four times as strong. In fact, True Blue for me goes hand in hand with Like A Virgin. Both are superb achievements, and though she has moved on by the time of True Blue, the album is not a massive leap as Like A Prayer would be three years later. Just as iconic (the Herb Ritts cover remains one of the most defining Madonna images there is) as the previous record, or perhaps more so, it also has the equal amount of heaviness and light fun, both delivered in healthy doses.

But with True Blue she reached a height she never would again, commercially at least, with a ludicrous amount of sales that very few people could hope to equal. The 25 million and counting seems ridiculously unachievable these days, but True Blue stands for a time when stratospheric sales were a possibility. It is also, sales aside, a very fine album, a feel good record that has hardly aged at all; nostalgic and urgent at once.

Reviewers at the time often used the word "canny" in regards to Madonna, a description they would certainly not fire at her male counterparts Michael Jackson and Prince, who would just be called successful, plain and simple. But critics saw Madonna's moves as cynical and calculating. There might be truth in the fact that Madonna knew what would sell, but at the same time, calculation and sexual manipulation do not shift 25 million units - good songs do.

In their original review, Rolling Stone mirrored many male attitudes towards Madonna's music. "If there is a problem with Madonna's proke-rock testament, it's the lack of outstanding songs. Only the magnificent Papa Don't Preach — Madonna's Billie Jean — has the high-profile hook to match Like a Virgin, Dress You Up and Material Girl. Not coincidentally, all of the above were written by outside contributors. White Heat, Jimmy Jimmy and World Go Round are excellent within their aspirations and easily comparable to Angel and Holiday (though not quite up to Into the Groove or Lucky Star). But none has the feel of a pop event. Party starts well but doesn't ignite, and True Blue, a cross between Heaven Must Have Sent You and Chapel of Love, squanders a classic beat and an immensely promising title. In commercial terms, it may not matter. Live to Tell hit Number One on career momentum, and Papa Don't Preach is great enough to carry several of True Blue's solid contenders home. In a clever double-entendre, M. — no longer anything like a virgin — pleads for her father's approval of the decision to keep an unborn child. Given Madonna's conscientiousness and ambition, it's not likely True Blue's dearth of "career records" was intentional. But its integrity and very freedom from attention seeking may turn out to be yet another piece of great timing in a remarkable career. Madonna's sturdy, dependable, lovable new album remains faithful to her past while shamelessly rising above it. True Blue may generate fewer sales and less attention than Like a Virgin, but it sets her up as an artist for the long run. And like every other brainy move from this best of all possible pop Madonnas, it sounds as if it comes from the heart."

Quite why so few writers wanted to recognise Madonna as a talented songwriter and creative force is a question for the ages, but one must blame rampant sexism. Because Madonna looked and acted a certain way, in their minds it could not also mean she was a serious artist capable of making terrific music. But True Blue spoke - and indeed speaks - for itself, and though she had a lot of help in its creation, it remains very much *her* piece of art, *her* statement, and *her* album.

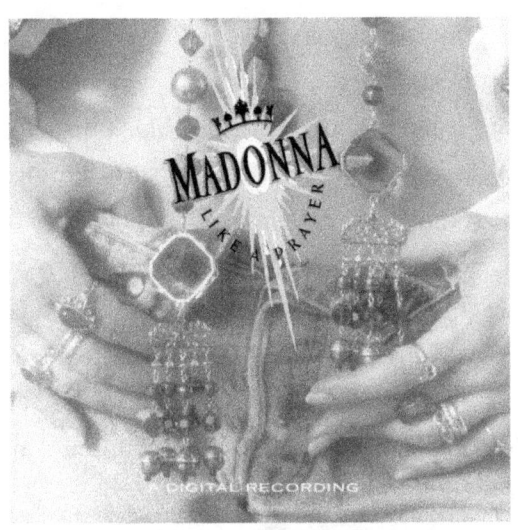

LIKE A PRAYER
BEST ALBUM OF THE 1980s?

"Like a Prayer is about the influence of Catholicism in my life and the passion it provokes in me. In these songs I'm dealing with specific issues that mean a lot to me. They're about an assimilation of experiences I had in my life and my relationships. I've taken more risks with this album than I ever have before, and I think that growth shows."
\- Madonna

Madonna's three studio albums prior to the release of Like A Prayer (not counting the remix record You Can Dance or her four songs on the Who's That Girl soundtrack album) certainly had their own varied set of moods and styles, ranging from rabid disco pop to moody ballads. None of them however, felt as naked, daring and exposed as her 1989 masterpiece Like A Prayer, a record which went from dazzling heights of bubbly self empowerment (Express Yourself), through powerhouse anthems (the title track), child like fantasies (Dear Jessie), heart breaking ballads (Promise to Try) to painful autobiography (Oh Father). Nearly thirty years on, Like A Prayer reminds a towering achievement, one of the most bare, brave and defiant albums ever released by a mainstream artist. Always honest, at times avant-garde and challenging, it's arguable whether she or anyone in the pop/rock field got close to this level of quality ever again. Moving, powerful, haunting, uplifting, appealing and warm, it manages to be all this and much more.

The year of 88 had been relatively quiet for Madonna, and though she did act on Broadway in Speed the Plow, she did not record any new music. It was a turbulent time for her. She split with Sean Penn and reached the not unremarkable age of 30, the age her mother had been when she died. It was time for some soul searching. She headed for the studio and began writing songs with Patrick Leonard. Leaving the fun teen sound behind her, Madonna was maturing - and so was her audience, and she was very aware of this fact.

"She'd start writing lyrics and oftentimes there was an implied melody," Leonard later said of the process they had on the album. "She would start with that and deviate from it. Or if there was nothing but a chord change, she'd make up a melody. But, a lot of the time in my writing there's a melody implied or I even have something in mind. But she certainly doesn't need that. She would write the lyrics in an hour, the same amount of time it took me to write the music, and then she'd sing it. We'd do some harmonies, she'd sing some harmony parts, and usually by three or four in the afternoon, she was gone".

"Sometimes, the music is sort of there," Madonna told Interview Magazine in 1989, "already written by either Pat Leonard or Stephen Bray. They give it to me and it inspires or insinuates a lyric or feeling. Then I write out the words in a free form, and we change the music to fit the form. Other times I'll start out with lyrics, or I'll have written a poem and I'll want to put that to music. Then I end up changing the words a little bit to make them more musical. Sometimes I'll hear the melody in my head. I don't write music and I don't read music, so I'll go to Pat Leonard, who is an extremely talented musician, and I'll sing it to him and make him play it, making chords out of it. Then I write the words to the song."

The first song they came up with was the immortal title track, from the word go a contender for Madonna's most powerful song yet. It begins and consistently feels like a hymn, with Madonna at her most holy, the music backing her up and doing service to the song and her voice. She speaks from within and the results are pure, mercurial, dazzling even. Though she had already recorded her fair share of classics, it feels like Madonna Ciccone has arrived.

"Well, originally, when I recorded the song," Madonna said, speaking of what the song was to her originally and how it became the anthem it is, thanks in part to the groundbreaking music video, "I would play it over and over again, trying to get a visual sense of what sort of story or fantasy it evoked in me. I kept imagining this story about a girl who was madly in love with a black man, set in the South, with this forbidden interracial love affair. And the guy she's in love with sings in a choir. So she's obsessed with him and goes to church all the time. And then it turned into a bigger story, which was about racism and bigotry. I wanted to put something in about Ku Klux Klan, use burning crosses... but then Mississippi Burning came out and I realized I was hitting the nail on the head a little too hard. Too obvious. So I thought I should take a slightly different approach. My original idea was much sadder. Kind of: this is reality, and reality sucks."

Like A Prayer is as perfect pop can get, a stirring, emotional and dramatic song which although majestically worked out, produced and played, also still manages to feel soulful, from the heart, and exciting, spontaneous even. The music is simple, never over fussy and the choir fit the arrangement tastefully, but it is still Madonna's voice which sticks out the most, and to whom the focus almost automatically veers towards. She is at her best here, hitting the top and bottom of her vocal abilities, scaling the heights she is capable of and taking herself to areas she hadn't before. It's a revelation.

"Pat had the chord changes for the verse and the chorus.," Madonna explained in 1989. "We hadn't written the bridge yet. I really wanted to do something really gospel oriented and acapella, with virtually no instrumentation, just my voice and an organ. So we started fooling around with the song, and we'd take away all the instrumentation so that my voice was naked. Then we came up with the bridge together, and we had the idea to have a choir. In almost everything I do with Pat, if it's uptempo, there's a Latin rhythm or feeling to it. It's really strange."

Express Yourself, though much lighter, is just what is needed after the weight of the opener. It's guilt free danceable fare, and Madonna brings in the cheer just as she had on her three previous albums. Any

Madonna fan who might have been surprised by the dramatic opener must surely have sighed in relief that their pop queen had not abandoned them fully, and still knew how to have fun. The great thing about Madonna's 80s album is the shifts in moods, rather like the way a Beatles record used to skip and hop from style to style almost effortlessly without ever causing the listener any concern. Like A Prayer is very much the same, going from dark to light in an instant.

Love Song is legendary in the fact it combines Madonna and Prince on record, though it often feels more like Prince's baby and is not as focused as the stronger Leonard and Bray co-writes. One cannot help but feel slightly underwhelmed by the results of this pairing, two of the heaviest legends of the 1980s no less. The track's rather slight air might be down to the fact that for once, Madonna could not fully have her own way. Maybe she is at her best when totally in control, and Love Song does sound more Prince than Madonna.

"We sat down and just started fooling around," she said of the song's birth. "We had a lot of fun. What happened is that he played the drums and I played the synthesizer and we came up with the original melody line; I just, off the top of my head, started singing lyrics into the microphone. And then he overdubbed some guitar stuff and made a loop of it and sent it to me, and then I just started adding sections to it and singing parts to it. And then I sent it back to him, and he'd sing a part to it and add another instrument and send it back to me...it was like this sentence that turned into a paragraph that turned into a little miniseries. So it was great. It was a completely different way to work. And because of our schedules and everything, and he was in Minnesota and he likes to work there and I like to work here. So we kind of sent it back and forth. He's great. He's a real interesting... unique talent."

Til Death Do Us Part is much better, a pained and painful examination of a marriage heading for disaster, spinning recklessly into oblivion, lovelessness and, most disturbingly of all, violence and abuse. Madonna sounds vulnerable, hurt and damaged, but never beaten or defeated. The lyrics sting and Madonna's voice sings them with sincerity. The harmonies are wonderful, and the music has such a joyous, bubbling bounce to it than one almost forgets the true weight of the song itself when focusing merely on the sounds, the musicianship and the fine production. But this is one of Madonna's most serious and raw songs, a stinging, slightly uncomfortable trip into a dangerous relationship. You can almost feel the bruises forming.

The album continues in its relentless power with Promise to Try, a beautiful, stripped, exposed ballad, with Madonna singing over a piano and little else. It remains one of her most stark songs. Her vocal efforts are wonderful here, and there is a true beauty in her voice which slaps down any doubters who accuse her of not being able to sing. When asked if Promise to Try was written for the little girl in her, Madonna revealed a certain vulnerability. "Yes. It was...yes, it was. I mean, it's not just one thing. It's my father talking to me, it's me talking to me... and Oh Father is not just me dealing with my father. It's me dealing with all authority figures in my life."

With songs like this, it makes you wonder why anyone would not only dismiss Madonna's music, but choose to side line it so often in favour of the image and the tabloid shenanigans. Speaking to Song Talk in 1989, Madonna finally had the chance to point out how the public Madonna often overshadowed the artist. "The image gets in the way," she bluntly said. Song Talk also gave Madonna the opportunity to actually talk about her latest album, the creative process and how she wrote songs on a basic level. When the interviewer expressed surprise over the fact that Madonna wrote so many of her songs, she was clearly irritated. "You mean they don't realize I'm a songwriter as well as a slut? (laughs) It's the image that gets in the way. What am I supposed to do? The information is on the label. If they don't read it, that's not my problem. I'm not going to put a sticker on the outside of the album that says, "Listen – I wrote these songs!" You know, they pay attention to what they want to pay attention to."

She also explained the tone of the Like A Prayer album, and where the approach came from. "I didn't try to candy coat anything or make it more palatable for mass consumption, I guess. I wrote what I felt. It's not that I candy coated it (before). I just chose to write in a certain vein. It's like anything – it's like movies: There are brutally honest, frightening movies and there are really slick, commercial films, and I like both of them as long as they're well made. 'm constantly inventing scenarios that are a combination of something I know and something I imagine. But it's just a side of myself that I chose to show. I definitely have that slick, glamorous, manufactured side that I feel very comfortable with showing to the public. But there's the other side to me, too. In the past I wrote a lot of songs like that, but I felt they were too honest or too frightening or too scary and I decided not to record them. It just seemed like the time was right at this point. Because this was what was coming out of me. I wait for inspiration. I set out to record an album and that was my state of mind at the time."

Cherish is pure joy, a bouncy number which lifts the album back into joyous pop, and out of the weighty depths of introverted autobiographical cleansing, which we the listener can happily bathe in for hours. It comes at just the right time, and though not shallow in the slightest, it's fun, light and refreshingly devoid of heaviness. It could have, in fact, come off any of her three previous records, and that of course is not a bad thing in any way.

Dear Jessie is purely magical, a tribute to Leonard's daughter who hung around the studio a lot during the making of the LP, and who Madonna got very close to and fond of. Her innocence became infectious, and Madonna was once again, like on Promise to Try, back in touch with the little girl within her. Given a George Martin-like Beatles orchestral score, the song is a mini masterpiece, another breathtaking and surprising addition to this varied and versatile album. It segues calmly into the dark beauty of Oh Father, which begins with cinematic strings which rise to a shiver inducing opening Madonna line - "It's funny that way." So begins one of Madonna's most musically rich, lyrically complex and neatly constructed songs.

"My favourite thing that we ever recorded, ever -- or wrote -- is Oh Father," Leonard later said. "That to me is the best thing we ever did. So, it didn't surprise me because we knew when we did it, that there was something about this that was in a way kind of the most *real* thing. [For] that song, the 'record' button was only pressed three times. It was pressed to do the track, live, with her singing live. Then we did the orchestra. And then we did a double of her vocal when we were mixing. That's it. So it's real. It's something that I really wanted to do and she was kind enough to say "let's try this," and it was not easy. There's two or three guitar players playing. I'm playing keyboards. Jai

Winding was playing keyboards. There was a percussionist and a drummer -- and she's singing -- all at the same time. These days, people go 'wow, that seems crazy.' Those days it wasn't uncommon for everybody to be playing together even though you're not a band. But it was one of those things where the arrangement was tricky enough, that it really took some working out to get it all right. Even all those weird synth overdubs and things -- all those things were being done live. We worked out all the parts, had all the sounds. I remember that we cut it live, and then put the orchestra on. You're not doubling the orchestra, so it's one pass for the orchestra."

The run of emotive songs here is really quite stunning. When you take the album in on headphones, shutting out the world around you, you find yourself drifting off into her painful, bitter sweet and overwhelming journey. According to the singer herself, it was "my attempt to embrace and accept my mother's death." Once again, tragedy inspired truly great art.

Keep It Together is more upbeat and one of the breeziest moments on the whole record, with its funky slap bass and energetic musical arrangement. Written by Madonna and Bray, it's sonically happy but hides a deeper message about not forgetting the importance of family. Prince adds some nice guitar work in here, and there are some nifty Madonna backing vocals. It was also released as a single and got to number 8 in the US charts.

The exotic Latin element returns to the fore, as it had on La Isla Bonita, with the truly wonderful Spanish Eyes. Like Oh Father and Promise to Try, the song is driven by a stirring and unforgettable piano melody, which couples itself closely with a pure and fiery vocal from Madonna. Although many say she only truly expanded her voice on the Evita soundtrack album (the 1996 movie where she played Eva Peron and won a Golden Globe), I feel that she moved up a gear with this album. As the material was so emotional and came from a darker place within herself, she undoubtedly got more entangled in the work, and externalised those inner demons of catholic guilt and the sadness brought on by her mother's death. It's there in the voice, the cracks, the tiny flaws, and in her artistic honesty. There are some brilliant Mariachi trumpets here too, and a strong piano backdrop over which Madonna sings her heart out.

The final track is Act of Contrition, a pretty free and avant-garde moment on this otherwise finely arranged and mapped out album. Featuring Madonna reciting the Catholic prayer over a chorus of whoops and hollers, not to mention tracks from the album played backwards and some shredding guitar solos, it's up there with The Beatles' Revolution 9 for its sheer bravery. Indeed, the backwards music and spoken word segment is very reminiscent of what the fab four were exploring and playing around with at the back end of their career, both as a group and singular entities, and it's little wonder that the scale and variation so evident on the Like A Prayer album caused critics to compare her to The Beatles. She was doing in her time what they had done in the 1960s; she was dominating music, popular culture and much of the tabloids, all the while advancing pop beyond its limitations (largely forced upon it by industry suits) and enhancing it as an art form, while of course being one of the most popular and highest selling pop acts of the day - pretty remarkable when you think about it.

The success of Like A Prayer was, by anyone's standards, absolutely huge. Selling 15,000,000 copies upon release (it's probably double that now to be honest) and spawning six hit singles, it was not quite as big as True Blue, but the acclaim was unprecedented. Though some were still untrusting of her supposed audience manipulation and endless drive for success (and more of it), no one could accuse her of phoning it in and merely making a passable record. Indeed, it was clear from every song, every word, every note, that she had invested as much of herself in this album as was possible. Not only that, she had dug so deep within herself that she found aspects so buried that she hadn't even known they were there. This was art, dressed and packaged as pop, but no less a work of art because of that.

When you judge the album to what else came out at the time, you see how remarkable Like A Prayer still is today. Comparing it to Michael Jackson's Bad for instance makes for interesting results. Bad was a stylistically rich album, full of great songs but very little, if any, bare emotion. It was a pop through and through, all echoey drums, catchy hooks, strong choruses and plenty of typically Jackson-esque trademarks. In comparison, Like A Prayer is like a deep cut exposing the blood beneath the sheen surface. It feels like you are looking at a Van Gogh painting, relentless as it is in its exposition, boldness and inventiveness. Madonna had finished the decade off with an album few doubters would admit she had in her. Even now, it's rightly seen as some sort of pop zenith, a mountain every potential successor to her crown must judge their own work to - an ultimately fatalistic act I might add.

Rolling Stone were hesitant in dishing out any acclaim, still trying hard to dismiss her, but ultimately coming round to the album's undeniable merits. "Ever since Madonna's bellybutton first undulated its way into mass consciousness," they wrote, "her fame has been more a matter of image than artistry. Never mind whether there was any depth or resonance behind it; for many of her fans, the image alone — Madonna as wily, wanton boy toy, gleefully manipulating the material world — was resonant enough. For others, it was just an act, a coolly calculated pop ploy designed to sell records. With Like a Prayer, Madonna doesn't just ask to be taken seriously, she insists on it. Daring in its lyrics, ambitious in its sonics, this is far and away the most self-consciously serious album she's made. There are no punches pulled, anywhere; Madonna is brutally frank about the dissolution of her marriage (Till Death Do Us Part), her ambivalence toward her father (Oh Father) and even her feelings of loss about her mother (Promise to Try). Yet as intensely personal as these songs are, the underlying themes are universal enough to move almost any listener."

Their conclusion? "Like a Prayer is proof not only that Madonna should be taken seriously as an artist but that hers is one of the most compelling voices of the Eighties. And if you have trouble accepting that, maybe it's time for a little image adjustment of your own."

Madonna herself admitted as much, that the album was her coming of age artistic statement. "My first couple of albums I would say came from the little girl in me, who is interested only in having people like me, in being entertaining and charming and frivolous and sweet," she said to Interview Magazine upon the album's release. "And this new one is the adult side of me, which is concerned with being brutally honest."

Madonna was here after continuously brutally honest, and though she arguably never reached the heights of this again (I think she did in some ways, particularly on 1998's Ray of Light), she learned a lot from Like A Prayer; and so, whether we know it or not, did we.

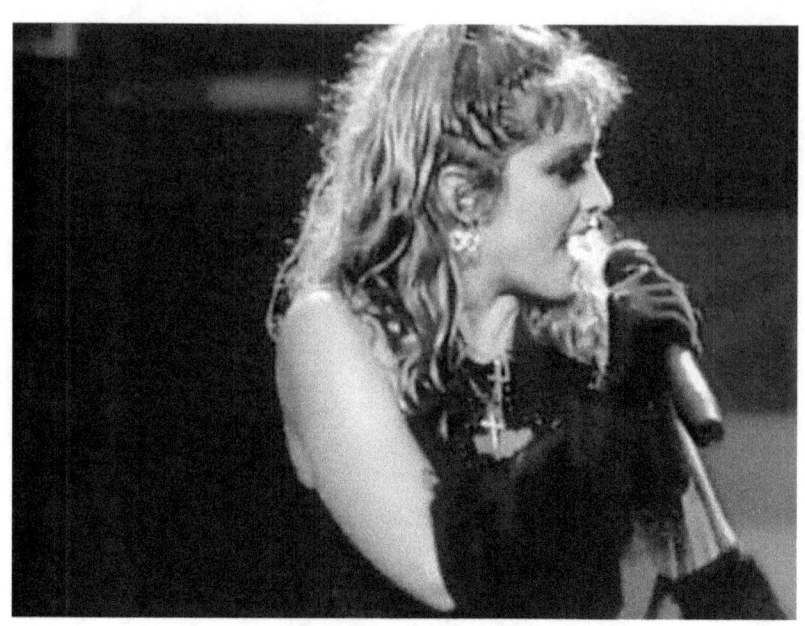

<u>EVERYBODY</u>

MADONNA AND THE FEMALE
ICONS OF THE EIGHTIES

It seems rather unfair and slightly disrespectful to discuss Madonna just in terms of her gender, as she has achieved more than most male singers combined too. But in this article, it is the key to truly understanding her phenomenal success in the 1980s by comparing her with her female contemporaries, not only to see what she was doing so differently to outsell them all, but also to see what she had to overcome in terms of sexism to get to the top.

The fact that she turned up in New York with 50 dollars and nothing but a whole lot of ambition makes you have even more respect for her. She wasn't paid into the business by a rich daddy, who forked out for decent professional demos, and she didn't have a family contact in the industry to move things along for her. No, Madonna had to eat out of bins, scrabble coins together to merely survive and sleep on couches and floors on her rise to the top. The fact she's ended up where she has is totally remarkable and unique. But there are other female artists who emerged around the same time who can be measured up to her, both artistically and commercially.

Yes, Madonna *can* be measured up to a small few female artists. A figure such as Kate Bush is one; but Bush, that British progressive artist who emerged seemingly from nowhere in late 70s Britain with a combination of clever song writing and amateur dramatics dance, definitely didn't have to eat out of bins on the way to success. A shy girl from the word go, she firstly played pubs as the KT Bush Band, before becoming a studio/album artist, save for one tour and a recent residency in London. She also came from a comfortable upper middle class background, where her talent was nurtured and encouraged (piano lessons etc.). Her father was a doctor and her brother knew David Gilmour of Pink Floyd. Bush's early demos reached EMI and eventually Bush got her contract without really having to do that much. Sure, she had the talent and the compositional skills, but her contact was what ensured the record deal.

Bush was born only one month apart from Madonna, so they are perhaps the two female artists you could compare to one another most realistically. Bush's masterpieces, like Hounds of Love and The Sensual World, are beasts all of their own, yet Madonna, an artist who began as pure pop and dance thrills, would mature at the age of 30 and cut a similarly gigantic album of influence and innovation, Like A Prayer. While both women had their teams, their helpers if you like, both are as head strong as each other. Of course, in other ways, they could not be more different. The retiring, almost reclusive family woman Bush became in the 1990s was a world apart from the sexually liberated, brash, in your face and utterly magnetic Madonna of the same era.

Like Bush though, Madonna emerged in the wake of punk and new wave. With her bands, Emmy and The Breakfast Club, she flirted with rock formats, but ultimately ended up surfacing as "Madonna" the boy toy, the care free disco princess of the mid 1980s. By this time, Bush was already very much the "serious artist" on a quest for perfection, getting closer to what she saw as the ultimate masterpiece, but never quite making it. Madonna, after she had dominated the charts with three consecutively effective studio albums - the first album, Like A Virgin and True Blue - achieved what many see as the zenith of 80s pop, Like A Prayer of course, her very own Hounds of Love. Sure, there are numerous differences between Bush and Madonna, but they also have a lot in common too. They are both powerful in very different ways and ensure they always get what they want. They have used sex, albeit VERY differently, to appeal to male audiences, but Bush has only really flirted with this area. Comparing her Babooshka video for instance, where she is clad in a skimpy warrior outfit, with Madonna's Justify My Love, and it's chalk and cheese. Bush goes around the edge, provoking but never shocking.

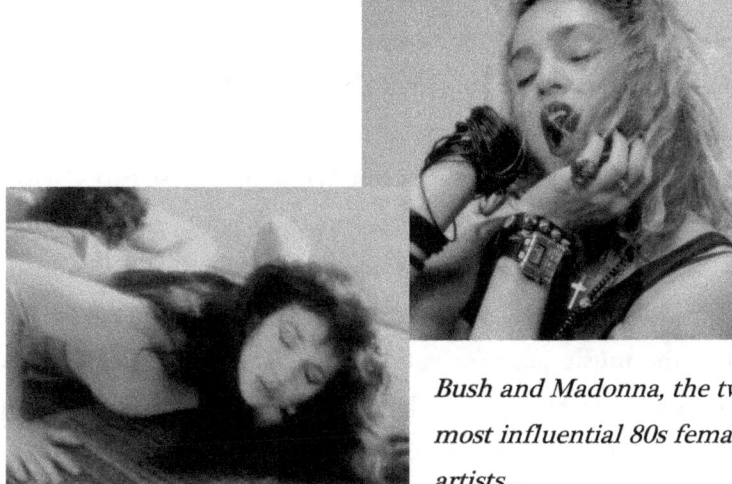

Bush and Madonna, the two most influential 80s female artists...

Madonna on the other hand, when considering also her innovative music video work, is full on, high on symbolism but not short of bare faced truths either. If you look at the albums, Bush's Sensual World is simply artsy poetics to Madonna's Erotica album, itself a fearless glimpse under the seamy, seedy bed covers.

Gig Wise pointed out Bush's influence on Madonna, but made the valid point that Madonna's imagery and lyrics set out to "shock instead of challenge." Of course this is arguable, as even Madonna at her most supposedly shocking definitely challenges the convention of the target and redefines it for all to see. It may take longer for people to notice, but in her time Madonna has changed a lot in art, not just for female artists, but for everyone.

In an article for New York Magazine, Ben Williams focused on the release of both Bush and Madonna's 2005 albums, Aerial and Confessions On A Dance Floor respectively, twenty odd years since their rise to fame. "Madonna and Kate Bush lord over opposing constellations in pop's cosmos: the deity of public materialism versus the divinity of private mysticism," wrote Williams. "These two 47-year-olds have had oddly parallel careers, emerging onto their respective scenes—post-disco New York and post-prog-rock England—in a blaze of sex and self-sufficiency, trailblazing paths that barely existed for women in the music business before them. The house of Madonna has given us Gwen Stefani, Peaches, and Britney. The line of Bush descends to Sinéad O'Connor, Björk, and Tori Amos. Now both singers have comeback albums of a sort—in Madonna's case, after an experimental, poorly reviewed album and tour; in Bush's, after a twelve-year maternity leave. Both are a return to roots, and to a kind of rapture—that of the dance floor and the English countryside, respectively. But they represent rather different responses to middle age."

Going on, he seems to be comparing both artists and competing them against each other, which seems rather odd when you consider how many differences there are between the thoughtful subtlety of Aerial and the care free shameless thrills of Confessions. However, he does conclude his piece with an interesting idea, putting Bush's settled middle age motherhood against Madonna's more urgent, jet set life. "Bush sounds incredibly contented, secure at the centre of her world," he writes. "You imagine her roaming around her country estate, occasionally dropping into the home studio to daub a dark accent onto track seventeen. It's doubtless a nice place to reach in midlife. But Aerial soundtracks bliss, rather than communicating it—what's needed is a little more of Madonna's restless spirit."

And "restless" is a key word for Madonna. She has tried every genre, every subject, every approach, every physical mage, every angle, every format, every possibility. Bush, contented and secure, is happy with her lot and will potter out to her home studio when the fancy takes her. Madonna though, is climbing ladders into attic studios, getting back to basics despite the fact she could book the priciest recording studio in the world for a year and not feel the pinch. This is the difference. Madonna craves to be at the hub of things, the epicentre of the hip, the "in" crowd and remain vital.

Bush is known for her perfectionism and eye for minute detail. She can spend half a decade on one record if she feels like it's necessary. Madonna, no slouch when it comes to recording as well as touring the globe, is already working on a follow up to 2015's Rebel Heart, itself following MDNA by a mere three years. That said, it doesn't mean Madonna rushes or compromises to get her work completed. Both artists toy with characters, play around with voices and get into their roles with passion and involvement. Bush is nutty on songs like The Wedding List (from the Never For Ever album), picking them off and loving every minute of it, while she even seems to channel her own inner Sparks on Violin from the same album. While her playful vocals soar and fly, they often seem contrived and forced, as brilliantly handled as they are. Madonna on the other hand, when settling into the Dita character of the Erotica album on its opening title track, does so effortlessly, whispering the text seductively and drawing you in, without feeling the need to perform vocal acrobatics and reach the highest possible notes. These are different approaches and totally opposing styles/genres/themes, but Madonna always seems more calmly immersed in her chosen roles.

But Madonna is a unique entity. As popular as she is (the most popular female artist of all time, no less), you have to wonder how she managed to shift so many units when releasing what is often quite avant-garde and challenging material. There is they key. Madonna, like Bush, retains all her artistic integrity and still manages to sell millions of albums. Bush is the artsy, surreal ponderer of womanhood, fantasy and relationships, while Madonna, not always subtle it has to be said, can take any theme on with the same amount of passion and effort. They both do what they do for themselves and would keep on doing it if five people were listening, never mind five million. In this way, they are very similar. It's worth noting too, that when Bush reappeared for her London shows in 2014, Madonna herself was present at one of the gigs.

Although the parallel similarities between Madonna and Cyndi Lauper have been pointed out many times before, a close inspection is always valid, for Lauper more than anyone has a lot in common with Madonna, both visually and musically. Both emerged in the New York music scene of the early 80s with a similar visual image, attitude and dress sense, and both released their debut in the same year, 1983. Their supposed rivalry was a big deal in the press at the time too, which makes comparisons between them even more tempting. Of course, this rivalry was totally fabricated.

"The media invented that rivalry," Cyndi later said. "We really didn't even know each other. We had a lot of friends in common, but we never really even met except for a few quick times at award shows. We both came out at the same time, we both were very into fashion, we were both very opinionated and demanded to be heard, but our music wasn't and isn't similar. They don't compare men who have successful albums in the same year, do they? When I became famous - I mean right away - the press always asked me about one person: Madonna. They tried to create this big rivalry, but my feeling was, you don't fucking knock another sister, ever. But even her record company got in on it. They ran an ad in Billboard where she was dressed in a white corset. And it said something like This girl gonna give Cindy Lauper a run for her money. I felt really bad about it. Everybody else was fuelled up by this supposed rivalry, but I was backing up, going don't wanna do this, I don't wanna be part of this. The thing was, our music wasn't even similar. Although if you ask me, her voice was sped up in Like A Virgin to make it sound high like mine. She was so smart about business and marketing (I never was) and she always was, and still is, beautiful. I kind of went the other way."

So if you look at the 1983 images of Madonna and Lauper, the truth is they are remarkably similar; the scraggly hair, the loose fashion, the eye catching appearance. But beyond that there is very little else. Musically, nothing linked Borderline with the likes of Time After Time (or indeed her defining hit, Girls Just Want to Have Fun). Later in the 80s, they became even further apart. Live To Tell and True Colors for example, two songs released by Madonna and Lauper in 86, could not have been more different, and by then, the two stars (five years apart in age, Lauper being the elder) were covering totally different ground to one another. Lauper had drifted out of serious contention by the late 80s and early 90s, and while remaining a valid artist, came nowhere near the dizzying commercial heights or creatively exciting zeniths which Madonna reached in that era. These days, Lauper is experiencing something of a renaissance. Her recent musical Kinky Boots won her an Olivier Award and not long ago here in the UK, she seemed to be just about everywhere. At the same time, Madonna has gone her own way, releasing albums and touring the world at a frantic speed, grabbing cover headlines and causing as much a stir as she ever has before.

There is more to the 80s though than a handful of female singers. Look at other female pop stars to come out and make it big in that time. Janet Jackson stepped out of her brother Michael's shadow and became a chart contender in her own right, but it was Madonna who arguably paved the way for her. She remained popular, and went on to push the boundaries in her pop videos, using sex as a tool for expression and shock. But was she an artist of Madonna's calibre, power and influence? Perhaps not.

So what is this about? Why compare Madonna with other 80s female pop stars you ask? Well, to see if she was a part of a musical movement. The truth is of course that she wasn't and never has been. She's Madonna, she is singular, existing in her own category. She cannot be lumped in with female pop stars of the age because she wasn't one. Like Kate Bush, she transcended music itself and brought pop to an art form. Unlike Bush however, and anyone else for that matter, she became so much more than music. She became a figure of hatred and adoration in equal measure, winding up as many people as she appealed to. She released good music, yes, but she also pushed buttons, pressed boundaries and challenged us all to sit up and pay attention to her. Why did she do it? Was it simply for attention? Maybe so. This aside, she made a monumental impact in those few years, broke taboos, ruled the charts and made her way as a household name.

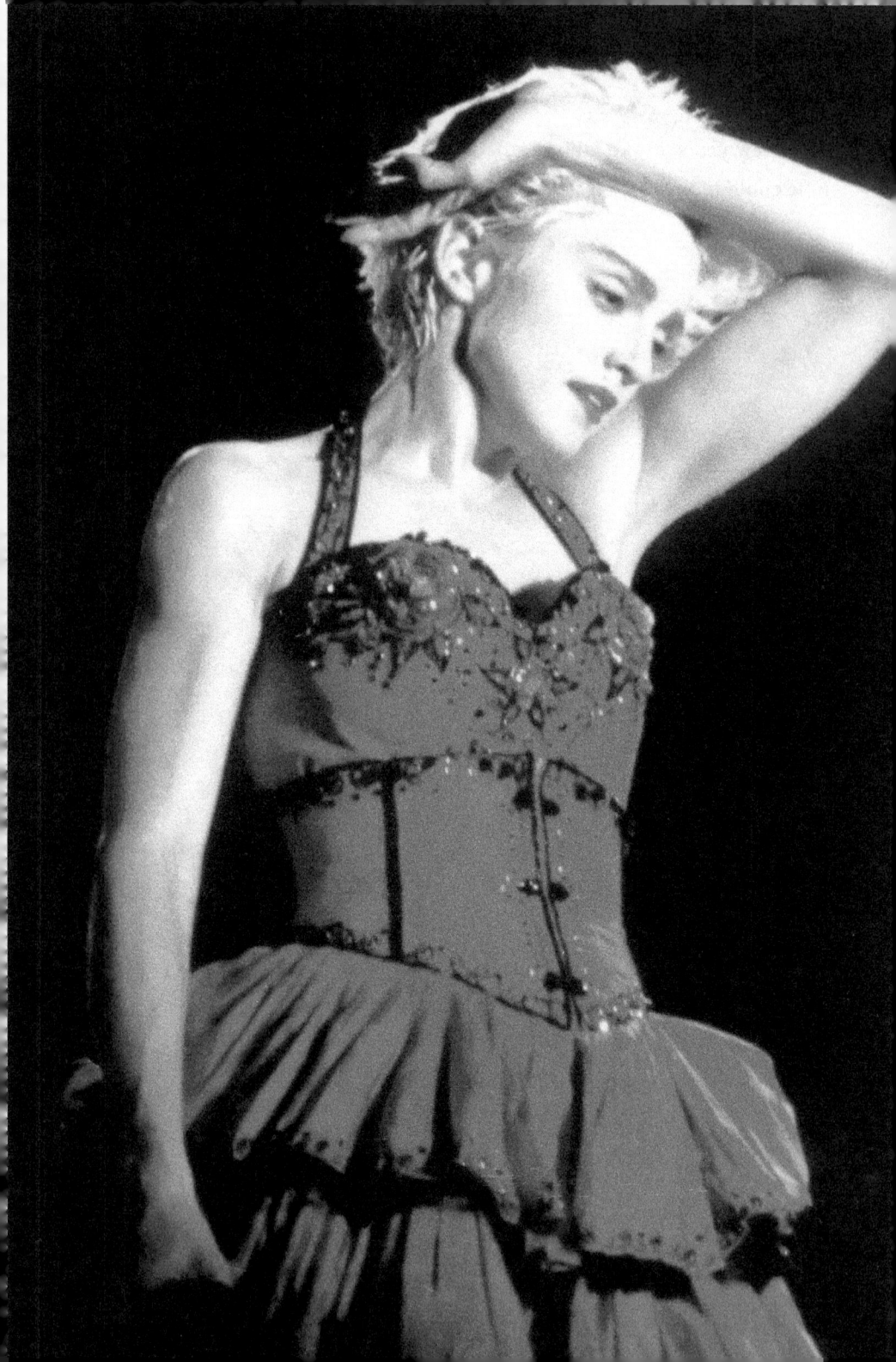

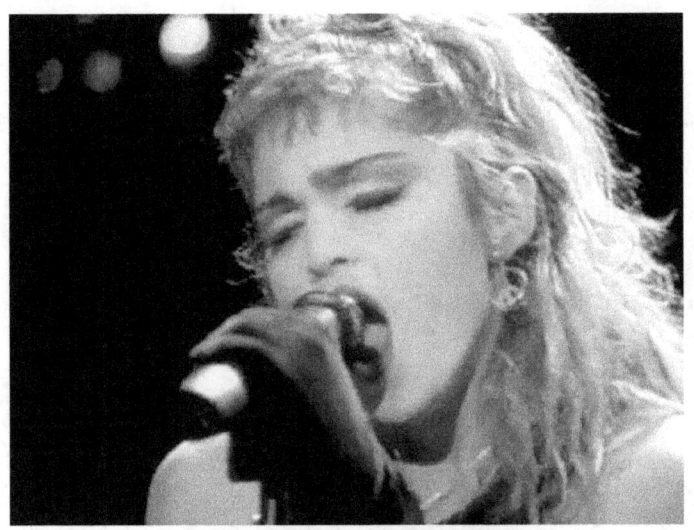

<u>ON THE STAGE</u>
MADONNA'S 80s TOURS

Though Madonna would undoubtedly go on to redefine and reshape what a live concert truly was in the 1990s and especially in the new millennium, even she had to start somewhere. While she has certainly made her mark in the recorded world (not to mention in the realm of the music video, a medium she helped define in the 1980s) Madonna has often said that the tours are, to her at least, her true artistic statement to the world, and are the place in which her creativity truly runs riot.

In 1985, it was announced that given the success of her first two albums, a live Madonna concert tour was on the cards. Given her huge popularity and record sales, a jaunt across the States on the stage was a no brainer. And so Madonna began to assemble a group of musicians, put together a set list and prepare her army to get out on the road, bringing the songs to the very people who had been supporting her over the past few years and buying her records.

The first tour was titled, quite simply, The Virgin Tour. It was announced on the 15th of March in 1985 and the excitement was immeasurable. When you consider that all Madonna's live shows

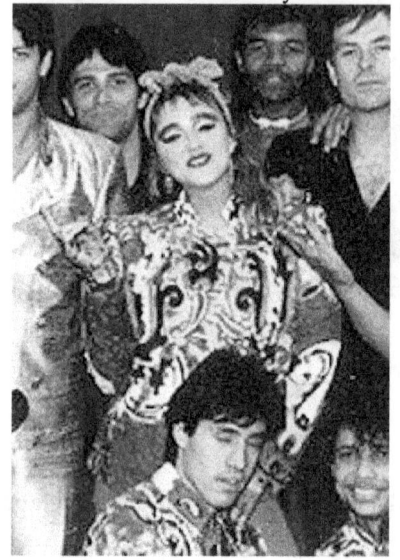

before then were in small clubs, and that Madonna had by that time released both her first album and Like A Virgin without any live appearances, one can imagine the sheer buzz and excitement of the build up, and of course of the shows themselves.

Madonna wanted the shows to basically be a "reflection" of her personality, what she called "loud and brazen," and her "DGAF attitude". It has to be said, the resulting show remains just that, a perfect embodiment of everything Madonna, at least the one of 1985, stood for. In outrageous, garish, extremely colourful outfits, Madonna took to the stage and went through her hits in a fairly straight forward manner, with backing dancers and a tight group propping her up. It was pop art unleashed, like an Andy Warhol painting coming to life before the eyes. Especially that bloody jacket!

As fun and spontaneous as the show looked, it actually involved a hell of a lot of planning on Madonna's part. "The most important thing was getting the band together," Madonna said in 1985. "I auditioned East Coast and West Coast musicians, and wherever the best musicians were, that's where I decided to set up shop. It just turned out that everyone in the tour was from Los Angeles. I brought out one guy from New York. It just so happens that's where I found the dancers too, though I auditioned dancers from everywhere."

Madonna began the tour in April at the Seattle Paramount Theatre, and worked her way through larger and larger venues across the USA. She ended up, two months later, with shows at Radio City Music Hall and Madison Square Garden. With Patrick Leonard and Billy Meyers on keyboards, other band members including Paul Pesco on guitars, plus two back up dancers (Michael Perea and Lyndon B. Johnson), the set was all about the songs, and their delivery was in your face, high energy and without distractions - save Madonna's outfits of course.

Thankfully for those who were unable to be there (I was a baby, and based in the UK) we have filmed evidence of just how good the shows were, and it has to be said, how direct they are in comparison to her later concerts. The VHS which saw release (still no official DVD of this yet) was recorded in her home town of Detroit, and has the hot young pop star at her early peak. There's a joyous, circus-like atmosphere, and everybody is there to party.

Dress You Up acted as the perfect opener, and on the recording one can see the excitement in the arena when the homecoming queen finally takes to the stage, the pop goddess they had all been waiting for. And though they said Madonna was not the best singer at the time, she actually sings very well, all the while dancing her heart out at the same time. It's a sublime performance, and every song is thrilling, enjoyable and wonderfully put across.

Holiday is a particular stand out, while Into the Groove is just as strong on stage as it is on record. There's a nostalgic glow to it all which takes you right back to your youth, from Madonna's sweet dance moves (she looks tiny in the footage), to the typically mid 80s music and her rather striking looks. Importantly though, the music on the tour stands up very well. The first album holds up as well as her more recent Like A Virgin LP, with strong renditions of Everybody, Burning Up and Lucky Star, not to mention a great Borderline. The highlights of the show though, for me at least, are breathtaking versions of Angel and Gambler, the latter taken from the Vision Quest soundtrack alongside Crazy For You. In all, the concert is stunning, illustrative of the fact that Madonna can hold the attention without back drops, projections, elaborate set pieces and dazzling lights (as great as they are, of course).

One thing which should be mentioned is how the show sells itself on two major elements; Madonna as a figure and the strong songs. It is also odd, for a Madonna concert that is, how it never gets involved in religious, sexual or sociological metaphors, as her later shows often would, and indeed still do. Though some critics argued that her ruling over the male dancers and the band had her as some sort of feminist supremo, and them as little more than underlings, this point seems rather simplistic and lazy in retrospect. Any pop star will undoubtedly be centre stage of their own show (after all, the punters paid to see *them*, not the backing dancers or session guys hammering away), so Madonna being the focal point of her own concert was hardly different from what Prince or Michael Jackson might gave done. On top of that, there was none of the camp, theatrical degradation or domination which Madonna would act out on dancers in her later tours (all in good fun of course), and there was an air of innocence about the whole thing. One can see many of the faces in the crowd are young, and no doubt impressionable, In retrospect, the Virgin Tour is remarkably clean, and the only provocative thrills come when Madonna removes her jacket, reveals her bra or shakes that famous belly. Otherwise it's family fun, clean as a whistle.

Still, reviewers at the time did not feel like focusing on the music, or the dancing for that matter, but instead ran straight to the "sex", which they saw as the show's main focal point and seller. Rolling

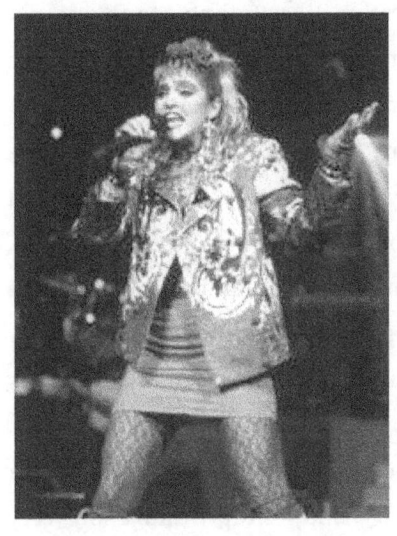

Stone wrote about her Seattle show: "Musically, the seventy-minute, thirteen-song performance was a satisfying, if unspectacular, re-creation of Madonna's records. One doesn't expect musical revelations from Madonna – and one doesn't get any. What Madonna is really about is sex, and there was plenty of that. The show began with glamorous close-ups of her projected onto five large screens that hung behind the band. Madonna then made her appropriately melodramatic entrance: a pink silhouette of her appeared on one of the screens, which rose, revealing the star, who descended a white staircase to the front of the stage, belting out Dress You Up. Wearing a kind of neo-psychedelic outfit – a coat embroidered with yellow-and-green and white-and-orange designs, a turquoise micro-miniskirt, a lace top, purple tights and black high-heeled boots – she looked like

Susan, the character she plays in Desperately Seeking Susan. Madonna's clumsy dance steps, funky costumes and camped-up-come-ons made her appealing and – surprise! – likeable. She's not some perfect, unattainable sexual icon; she's a real person, like her fans. (At least 80 percent of the girls had done their damnedest to mimic their idol's looks, from bleaching and tousling their hair to wearing such Madonna-associated items as see-through blouses, fingerless-gloves and crucifix earrings, which were on sale for twenty dollars in the lobby.)"

It was fairly obvious that a publication like Rolling Stone was not going to take much away from the music, and focus on the cynicism of Madonna being a lucrative product for the young girls who idolised her and dissected her every move. Yet while they have a point about Madonna's physicality and aura being central and essential to the show's success, the songs really do stand their ground, coming to life before the crowd, with Madonna's "imperfect" voice the perfect tool to belt them out. The musicianship is marvellous too.

Other magazines were more critical still, with New York Times taking the opportunity to attack her Radio City performance. "Because the fact of the matter was that Madonna – backed by a competent but rather ordinary touring band – simply didn't sing very well. Her intonation was atrocious; she sang sharp and she sang flat, and the combination of her unsure pitch and thin, quavery vocal timbre made the held notes at the end of her phrases sound like they were crawling off somewhere to die. In her high octave range, she had a more attractive sound, with just a smattering of street-corner edginess to it. But this woman needs to see a good vocal coach before she attempts another tour. And one hopes that the next time she

136

performs here, she will have learned not to toss tambourines into the air unless she's going to be able to catch them."

Variety were also a little mistrusting of her message. "But, for the most part," they wrote, "Madonna's singing was like a soundtrack to a more visceral display of herself, her persona, her nonstop dancing and her surprisingly explicit sexual dare, which included a visual climax – so to speak – to every song. Somehow, despite the hard-core moves, Madonna did not really come off as naughty or menacing so much as solicitous and good-hearted, a kind of flirtatious, sugary sex fairy whose outrageous poses were really just a gift for the kids, a fantasy offering to help them grow up. At show's end, Madonna made this explicit, revealing herself to be a good girl despite it all, following a coolly corrupt rendition of Material Girl with a surprising, almost plaintive question: 'Do you really think I'm a Material Girl? I'm not. Take it. I don't need money', she cried, tossing handfuls of play bills into the crowd."

The harshest criticism of these live shows unfortunately only mirrors the worst and most patronising reviews of her actual records, but these writers can perhaps be forgiven when you think that at the time of writing Madonna was a fairly new fad (despite numerous hit singles and two very successful albums) and hadn't had thirty odd years to prove herself and show she was a talented, smart and consistently growing artist in her own right (Not that even this fact has made the critics lighten their load on her at all). In 1985 she was still the care free Boy Toy, the midriff displaying party girl in control of her sexiness.

Asked by Molly Meldrum about the negative write ups of her shows, Madonna was confident. "Oh yeah sure," she replied, "That's

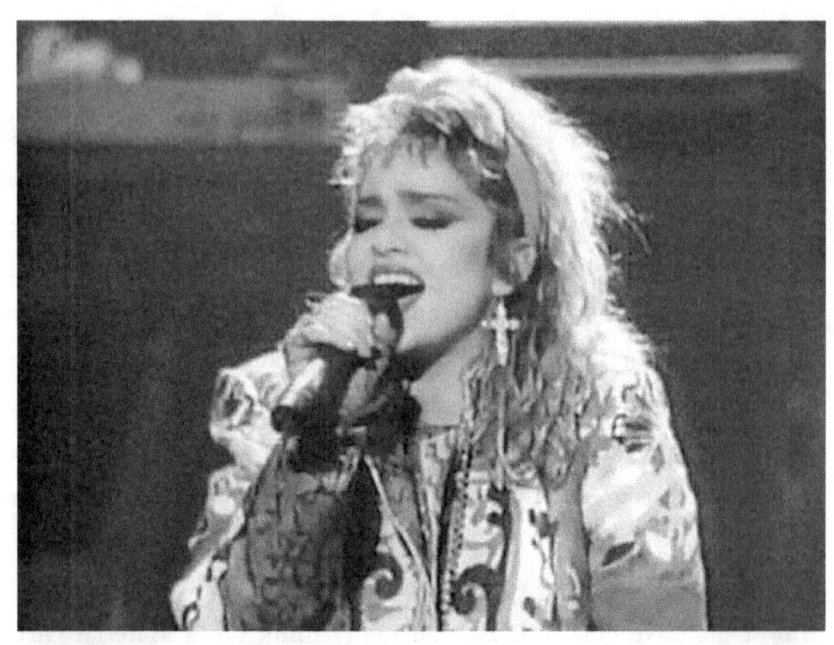

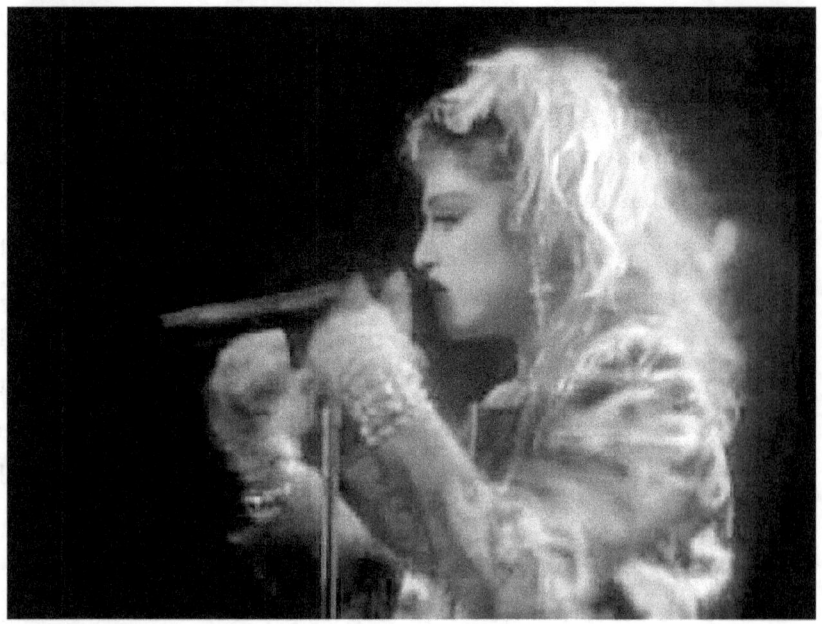

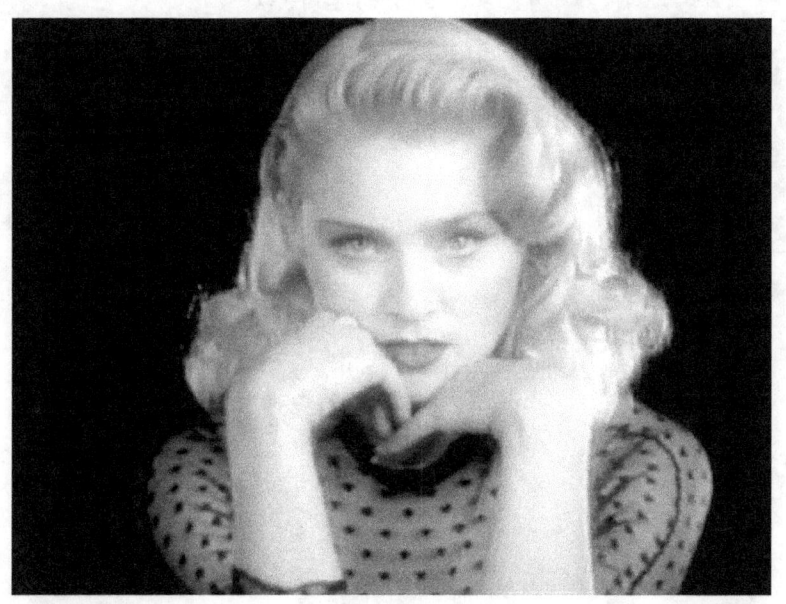

Above, Madonna advertising her Virgin Tour. Below, on stage.

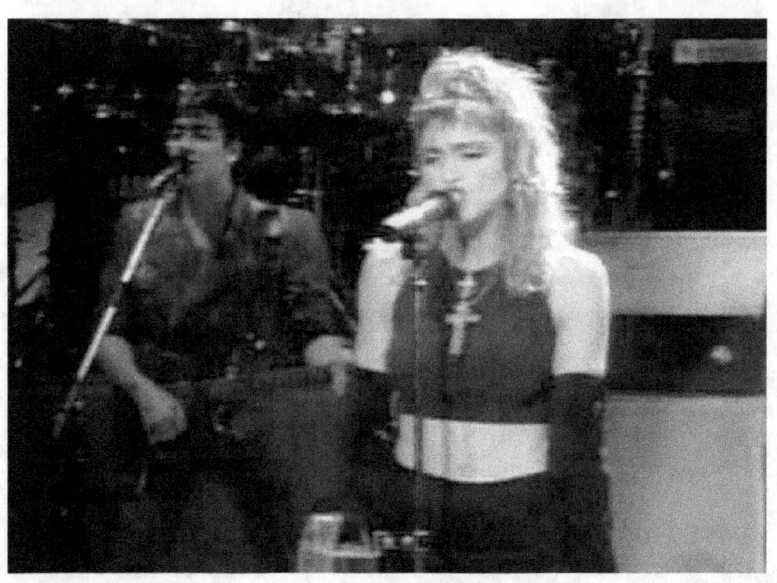

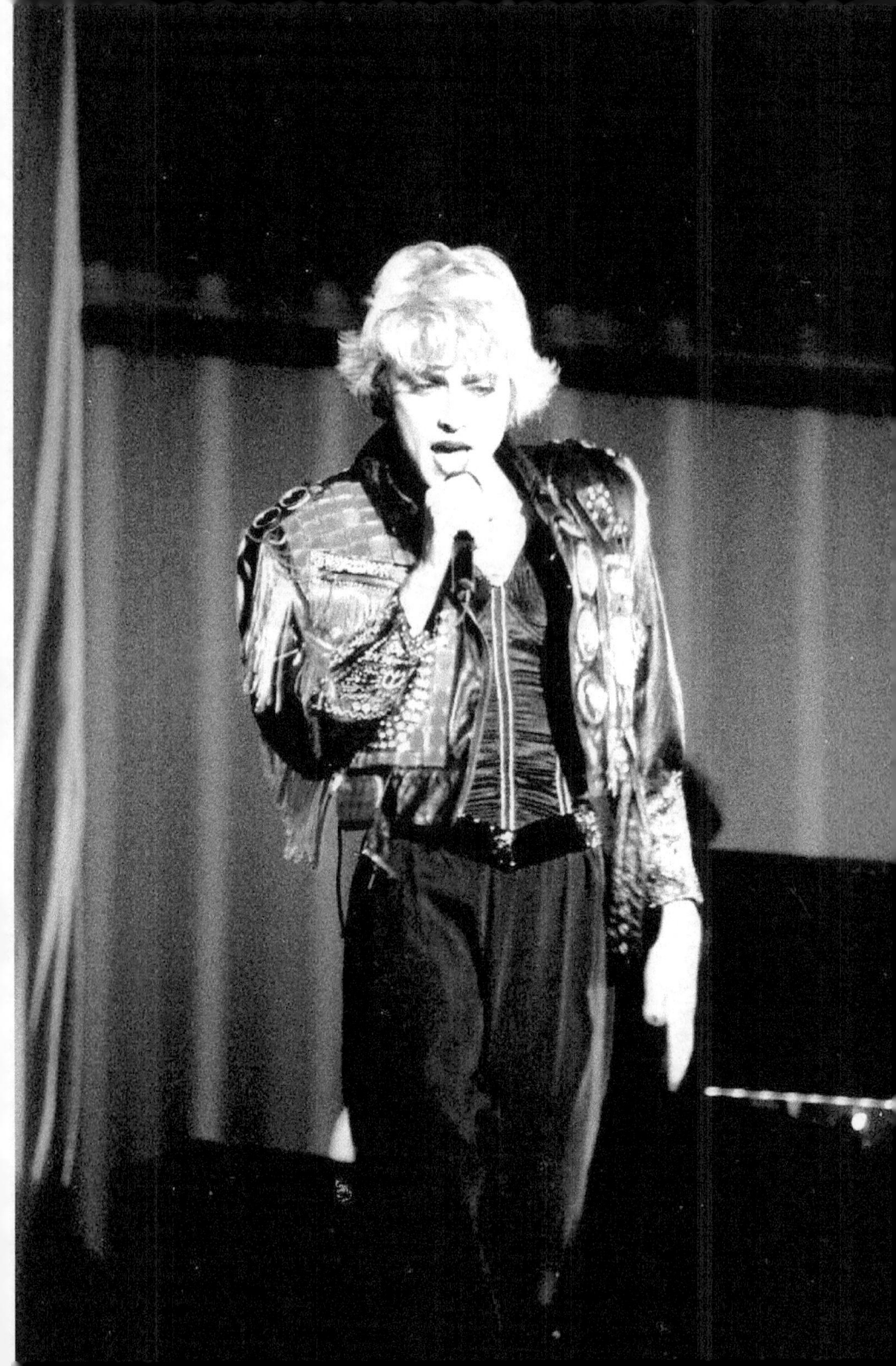

normal. Well, I think over all I ignored them because deep down in my heart I knew it was good. I knew there was going to controversy, and a certain amount of opposition to what I am doing."

Two years later, it was time to move things up a gear, and Madonna dove into another world tour. Though not on the scale of her tours in the new millennium, or even her Girlie Show and Blonde Ambition concerts (both in the early to mid 1990s), the Who's That Girl? tour was a step up into a new realm of scale. Madonna worked out obsessively for the show and got her physique to an almost athletic level. Gone was the midriff she so proudly displayed on the Virgin Tour (many writers had made big news of her so called belly, and she became rather obsessed with getting rid of it). Gone also were the long locks; her hair was now a cropped blonde, like some kind of new wave Marilyn Monroe. It was a drastically different girl from the Virgin Tour, that's for sure.

Jerome Sirlin was the set designer for the Who's That Girl? tour, a man who had already proved himself in theatre before meeting the Queen of Pop. Prior to getting the call from Madonna, Jerome told me recently that his work included "two performance works with Director George Coates, music theatre projects with Phil Glass, a sci fi music drama, and Hydrogen Jukebox."

On getting to work with Madonna, Sirlin told me, 'I received a call from Madonna... she had seen or heard of the 3D Holographic projection theatre I developed. We met up at my studio in the Village and discussed the Who's that Girl? Tour. I showed her 3D projection work in model form. I began listening to her song list and designing the tour shortly thereafter. I designed large format state of the art transparencies for the show and projected them in sequence, song by song, during rehearsals in a sound stage in Los Angeles. Basically, as in all musical productions I've designed, the projection design is based on an interpretation of the music and lyrics. I opened the tour and revisited it periodically during the tour. I recall showing her some of the 6" x 6" transparencies during rehearsals on the sound stage. After she rejected the first 3 or 4, I slowly closed the lid on the case of transparencies and told her to hold on rejecting them and to wait to see them projected on the full stage. She took my advice and liked the final result projected full stage. I learned to never present a project unless it was projected in a scale model or full scale."

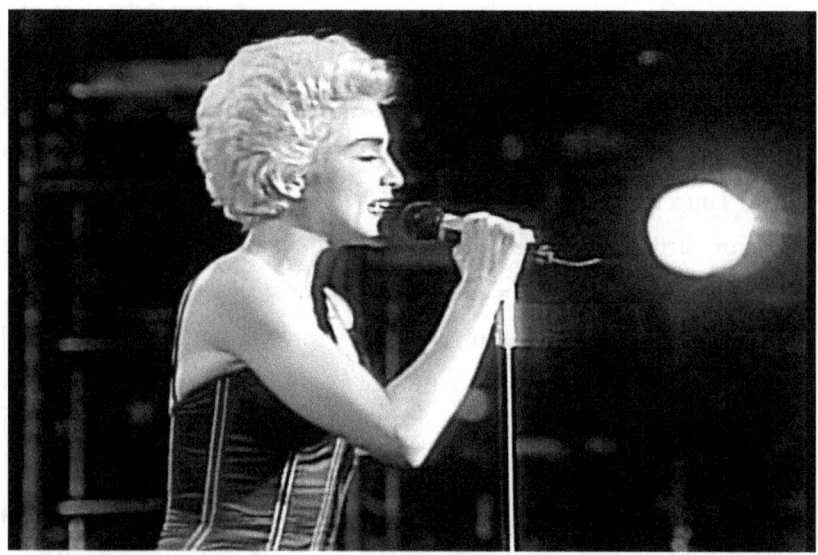

By Jerome's words it is clear that Madonna's perfectionism had truly arrived, and though the Who's That Girl? tour is as fun as the Virgin Tour, it does not feel as naive, innocent or wide eyed. It feels more worked out, professional, much more like the Madonna who strived for and achieved world domination. It is also, judging by the visual footage and audio recordings, a brilliant show from start to finish.

That said, the stripped down basics of the Virgin Tour were charming and instantly welcoming, and could not have contrasted more harshly with the costume changes and elaborate polish of the Who's That Girl? show. Clearly Madonna was more confident and intent on changing the idea of a live show. It was step one on her steamrolling path towards live concert domination, where all competition was forced to kneel before her and gasp at the extravagance, the sheer scale, and of course, the takings.

Still, even though this platinum blonde was commanding thousands of people at the time, she was not beyond nerves and insecurities. "I know that lots of people are paying attention to me and watching my every move," she said. "Also, I think I feel it more than ever now because I'm doing stadium shows and I get up on stage and I see 65,000 people all standing there and all of a sudden I feel like (sharp intake of breath) you know, I have a big responsibility."

Though the film of the same name was not a hit (Madonna claimed the tour took the attention away from the movie, and seeing as they both had the same name, caused much confusion with her fan base - which, to be fair, might just be the case) the tour certainly was, both money wise and artistically, a success. More polished and sure of herself, Madonna is a revelation in the footage. It also showed that Madonna was surer of her act, that she decided to head out of the States and tour Canada, the UK, Germany, France and, as documented on a live video, her ancestral homeland, Italy. With more back up dancers, singers and behind the scenes folk, the Who's

That Girl? tour was a lavish extravaganza. Perhaps she took note some of the critics' harsh put downs, and wanted to avert their attention away from her voice, which they were so sure was below par. By creating other sights and sounds on the stage, Madonna surely did not feel as exposed and vulnerable. She had a team up there with her,

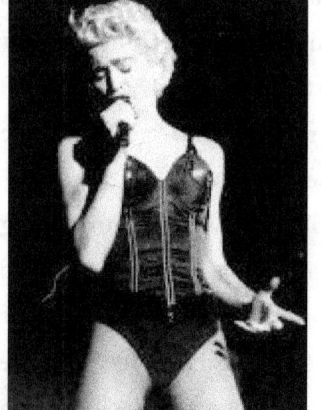 backing her every move.

Comparing this show with the Virgin Tour illustrates her speedy development. By 1987, Madonna is a completely different artist, and though there are some of the same songs, she has shifted immeasurably so in such a short time. A reinvention had occurred, to quote the often cited cliché.

Watching footage of the Italy concert and it's clear Madonna's show has become a frantic circus, and the reaction even to her silhouette during the opening of the first song, Open Your Heart, is ecstatic to the point of utter hysteria. It's Beatlemania all over again! (Did anyone coin the phrase Madonnamania?) When she first appears on the stage in her basque, straddling the chair as she did in the Open Your Heart music video, the screams are, to put it fittingly, wildly fanatic. Even watching thirty years on, on the limits of a TV screen, and you will find that the shivers go up the back. The excitement in the arena is almost too much to bear.

As for the music, it has the same excitement as it did on the Virgin Tour. Songs, again, are the key to the show's appeal, and they are performed tightly and efficiently; you cannot argue with that at all.

She brings cuts from the first record right up to 1987, with Lucky Star less a disco dance anthem and more a high energy, drum driven post-punk rocker. She also performs a particularly strong version of Papa Don't Preach, her voice sounding almost male in the verses, but soaring and affective in the chorus. Other overlooked gems like Causing A Commotion (from the Who's That Girl? soundtrack) and White Heat are wonderfully done too, sitting comfortably alongside Madonna anthems like Live to Tell, the perfect Into the Groove and the pure La Isla Bonita. And who can not love the hard rocking Holiday of this set? Taking in the aura of Madonna and the golden songs, it has to be said that watching the video gives you a warm glow - after all, you are experiencing 1987, and Madonna is on top of the world. Does it get any better than this?

Though the scale is huge, and indeed there are lasers, lights and projections, Madonna is still the main focal point, completely centre stage and it is impossible to take your eyes off her. There is still a sense of innocence to the show that it could appeal to all ages, young and old, which was missing from her equally brilliant but more mature Blonde Ambition, Girlie Show and even Rebel Heart tours. The music remains vital, bouncing and bubbly throughout, never letting up or sagging one bit. Costume changes are fast and somehow Madonna, only three years into her recording career, already seems like a veteran with a vast catalogue of hits under her belt.

She was well on her way to redefining the live tour, but on these two shows Madonna sold Madonna to a hungry public, and proved to them, and herself, that she not only a visual draw, but also a musical one too. The songs stand up, a fact which lesser people than you would think might point out.

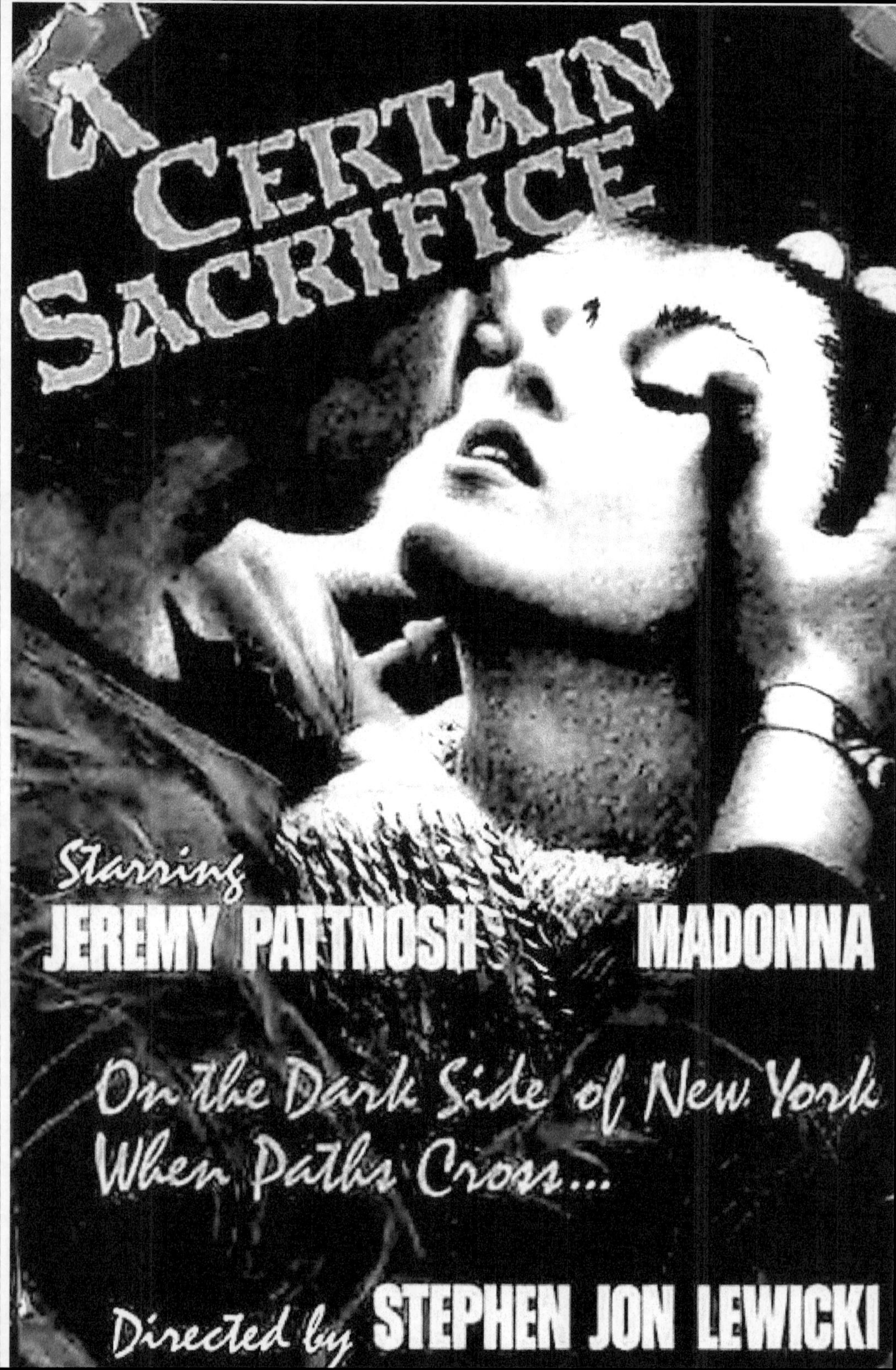
A CERTAIN SACRIFICE
Starring
JEREMY PATTNOSH · MADONNA
On the Dark Side of New York
When Paths Cross...
Directed by STEPHEN JON LEWICKI

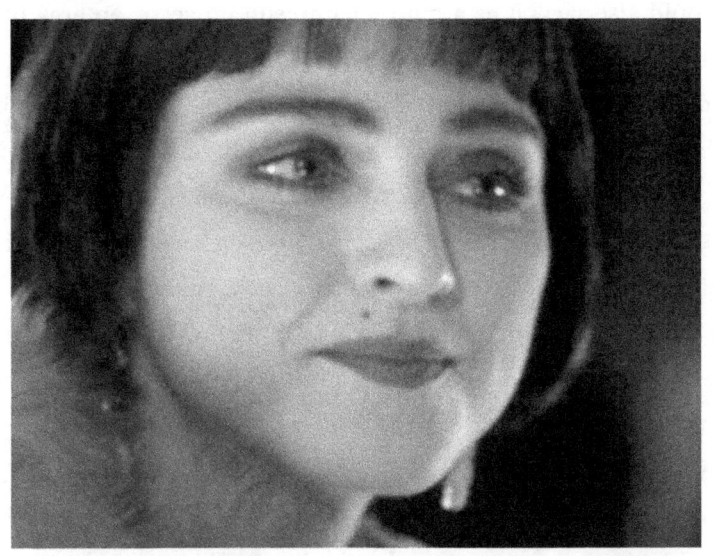

<u>MADONNA AT THE MOVIES</u>
AN OVERVIEW OF HER 80s FILM ROLES

OK, so these days, even to a large number of her fans, Madonna's film career is something of a joke. When comparing her acting aspirations to her monumental achievements as a recording, visual and performance artist in the musical field, the filmography in its entirety doesn't quite measure up, to say the very least. However, there are a couple of ways to view Madonna's film career that ensure it makes more sense as its own entity and a side arm to her main career, the day job as you might call it, as a hugely popular singer and entertainer. You can view it as a field where she definitely has talent, but has not always applied it properly to the film in question.

You could also view it as a highly camp sub universe, an area of her output that might not be perfect, but is definitely full of joys.

Madonna's film career in the 1980s was, in fact, not entirely unsuccessful when you take it all in and exclude it from the panned turkeys and missteps of the next decade, and indeed the one after. In the 1990s she did win critical praise for her work as the femme fatale Breathless Mahoney in Warren Beatty's Dick Tracy (1990), and was superb in a supporting turn as Mae "All the Way" in A League of Their Own (1992). However, as usual, it was the less than graceful film work people chose to bring up time and time again; like her darkly funny erotic thriller, Body of Evidence (1993) and the flop comedy Swept Away (2004), which she made with her then husband Guy Ritchie to international mockery. However, looking at Madonna's movie work in the context of the 1980s, alongside her music videos, concert tours and albums, the film work is good, at times very good indeed.

Madonna first acted, properly as you might say, in the student film project A Certain Sacrifice, directed by Stephen Jon Lewicki and shot in 1980. It didn't get released as such until Madonna was a star, five years later, and she objected very much to it going out on the market. But in truth there was actually little she could do about it, and in the mid 80s A Certain Sacrifice was a big seller on VHS, often promoted as an erotic thriller and a soft core flick, though it was really neither. It is, however, pretty bad and one can see why Madonna might be embarrassed by it. That said, she shines brightly in the grainy, seedy surroundings, and has a couple of interesting scenes. At the time of filming it though, she desperately wanted the role and even wrote the director a lengthy note saying as much.

148

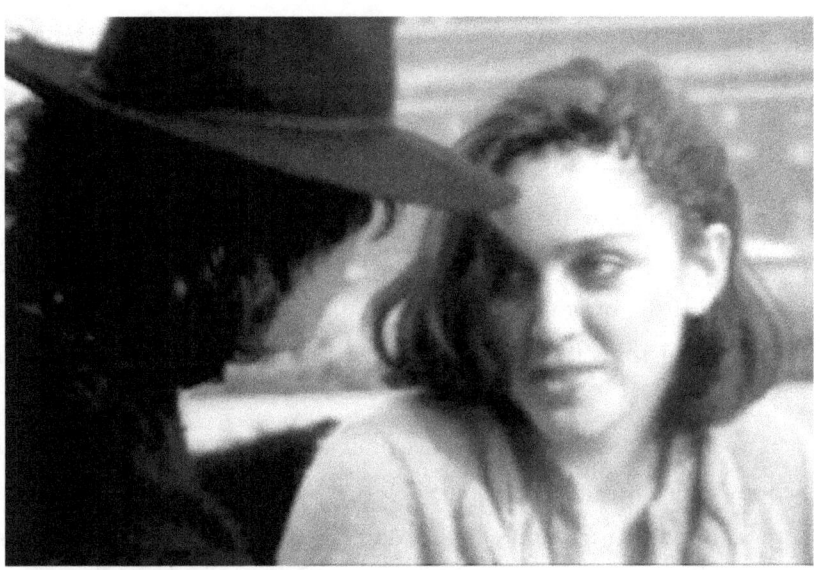

Madonna in her debut acting role, the film A Certain Sacrifice.

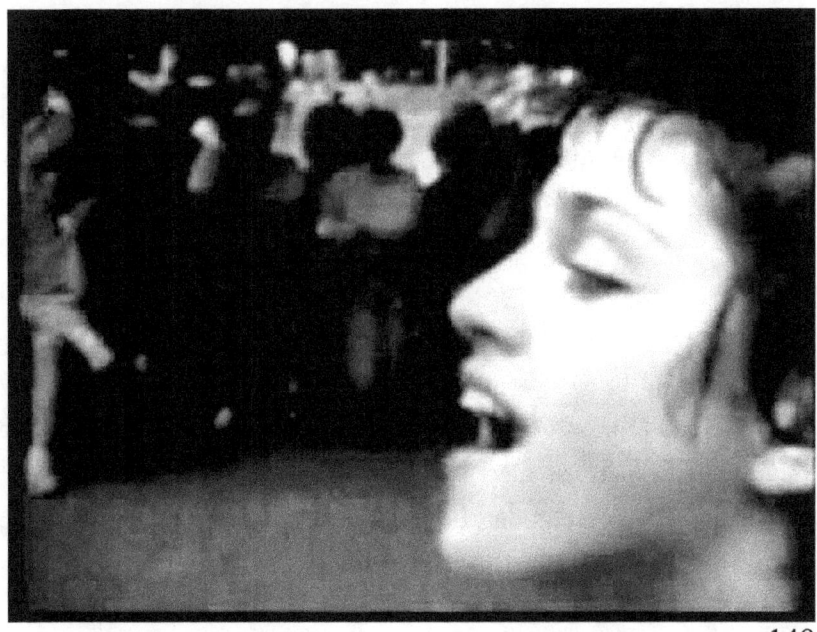

The release brought about trouble between Madonna and Lewicki. Initially she tried to buy the rights off him for $5,000, but he refused. After she tried to get it blocked, the pair sat down for a screening of the movie, after which Madonna stood up and shouted an expletive to the young director. Whether this is true or not is anyone's guess. So A Certain Sacrifice is the first screen credit. As it is though, no one can really call this her first starring role. The movie is hard to follow, and Madonna is the only positive thing in it, clearly trying her hardest to lift the thing from the gutter; even if she only achieves that feat with the scenes she is featured in.

"It was made by this guy in his final year at N.Y. University Film School," she told the NME in 1983. "It was sick in a childish kind of way, about this girl who's like a dominatrix, me of course. There's hardly any, like, sex scenes or anything like that, it's just implied all the time. She's got all these slaves, and she leads this really perverted, deranged life, but then this boy from the Midwest comes and changes her life, and makes her get rid of the slaves. Anyway, I get sexually attacked, which you don't see in the movie, and he goes crazy with revenge, kills the guy and performs this ritual sacrifice, gets all my ex-slaves involved. There's a scene where we take a bath in fake blood."

A Certain Sacrifice is not without merit though, and any devoted Madonna fan will want it in their collection. The weird "orgy" scene is reminiscent of things she might have done in the sex era, i.e. Justify My Love and Erotica, only in a much more muddled, shaky, primitive manner. Her performance is quite good too, and as a piece of evidence for how ambitious, daring and willing to anything at all to get noticed she was, the film is priceless.

Her first "proper" film role though, was 1985's Vision Quest, directed by Harold Becker. She had a small part as a club singer, and her scenes were featured in the promo videos for both Gambler and Crazy For You, put out as singles in 1985. Quite honestly, Vision Quest was your typical mid 1980s coming of age teen love story, starring 80s regular Matthew Modine. Save Madonna's brief appearances, the film has little going for it.

On the set of Vision Quest, Madonna spoke of her songs written for the film. "They wanted a slow love ballad, for when they're dancing. And that's exactly what the slow song is. The faster song, The Gambler, is really the girl's point of view; she doesn't really need this guy." Watching the seriousness of Madonna in the interview clip in question showed just how interested she was in the dynamics of film and she later admitted it was frustrating just playing the singer. "I wanted to be down there acting," she said.

"We shot it in Spokane, Washington," she told Interview Magazine. "It was very cold, lonely and boring. I do three new songs, two that I wrote and one other that's a ballad. Jon (Peters) and I met for another movie that he's producing, and when it came time for Vision Quest, they didn't want to get an actress to pretend she's a singer. They wanted someone with a lot of style already."

Madonna then emerged as a movie star in her own right, deserving full attention and acclaim in Desperately Seeking Susan, put out in 1985 to wild acclaim and good box office. In this energetic romantic comedy, Rosanna Arquette plays Roberta, a bored and frustrated housewife married to the wealthy Gary Glass (Mark Blum), but becoming increasingly dissatisfied with the soulless, suburban yuppy nightmare she is trapped in. Out of boredom, she's started to

151

obsessively read the ads in the New York papers and becomes particularly interested in one ongoing saga involving Jim and the free spirit Susan (Madonna), who goes all over the world from month to month living a glamorous life style. One day she reads a new ad which reads "Desperately Seeking Susan." When Roberta goes to the destination mentioned in the ad, Battery Park, she spots Susan. After buying Susan's jacket (once worn by Jimi Hendrix), she arranges another meeting at Battery Park. Later, Roberta is knocked out cold and wakes up with amnesia, and is mistaken for Susan. Meanwhile, some less than savoury types are searching for some stolen Egyptian earrings which Susan has in her trunk and the plot thickens.

It's a simple enough storyline, but little clever touches are added in to keep it fresh. Writer Leora Barish ensures the script never becomes saggy, filling it full of unexpected (and often comfortingly expected) plot twists and funny gags. Director Susan Seidelman keeps up the pace too, ensuring the farce moves speedily.

The part of Susan was one of the most battled for Hollywood female roles that year, even though the film was quite low in its budget. Originally, the producers saw this as a vehicle for superstars Goldie Hawn and Diane Keaton, but even by the mid 80s they were arguably too old to be playing the roles of Susan and Roberta. There were numerous other actresses up for Madonna's role, including, very nearly, Ellen Barkin, but it's hard to think of anyone else but Madonna in that part now. With her iconic jacket, endless outfit changes, huge trunk, dark sunglasses and care free attitude, this was a truly brilliant acting debut for Madonna, a role that was not unlike like herself (cocksure and confident), with just a little bit of bohemian flare added in (somewhat reminiscent of photos from her earlier rebellious days in bands). Her second album Like A Virgin was selling madly at the time of release. When she was originally cast however, she was not a huge mega star and her rise to the top coincided with the film's theatrical release, helping to make the movie a box office hit. After all, it was only a 4 million dollar film, relatively low budget by Hollywood's standards and had little riding on it.

"I had seen and loved Jacque Rivette's film, Celine and Julie Go Boating," the film's writer Leora Barish told me in 2015. "In it, an ordinary woman living an imaginatively very modest life sees a woman on the street - a chaotic, charismatic, mysterious woman - and simply gets up and follows her into an alternate reality which you feel is an invention of the strange woman's imagination. Together, they start to play with that reality. It's about playing and reality and women being the imaginative creators of their lives - a fantastic movie. A few days after I saw it, I noticed the personals in, I think, the Village Voice or maybe it was another paper, and the personals seemed to fit into a Rivette-like premise."

"This was my second film," Susan Seidelman said of the film and how she got involved. "I had done a low-budget independent film that was also set downtown, called "Smithereens," in 1982. And as a result of that, these producers, Midge Sanford and Sarah Pillsbury, sent the script to my agent. And I'm kind of a superstitious person so the Desperately Seeking Susan title caught my attention. It had that title already – that wasn't vanity on my part. But it had a theme that my first film was about. It's about finding out who you want to be and who you are inside. The inner Susan — the adventurous creature that's inside the suburban housewife — really interested me thematically. I wasn't a housewife but I grew up in suburban Philadelphia and I couldn't wait to cross the bridge, metaphorically speaking, into Manhattan. I just knew that there was something on the other side, out there, that I needed to get to."

On the casting of Madonna, Susan reflected, "Madonna lived down the street from me, so she wasn't 'Madonna,' in quotes. I knew her from people who were in the downtown music scene. We started to audition more up-and-coming actresses who had done some films -- people like Ellen Barkin and Melanie Griffith and Jennifer Jason Leigh and Kelly McGillis, who had just made one or two movies and were getting known. But even though the film is a fairy tale, in a sense, it needed to be grounded in some kind of authenticity. We didn't want actors putting on costumes and playing downtown. And she hadn't really done a movie before. She'd played in a band in the background of Vision Quest, whatever. But it wasn't really an acting role. I hoped that because she is a performer and she had such an interesting persona, I could capture that on film somehow. And that does involve a lot of acting. People sometimes think, Oh, it's just being. But it's not. When you have to say lines and hit marks and get your lighting and repeat it 20 times from different angles, it's acting. She had to do a bunch of screen tests. But it was the early days of MTV, and she happened to have a video that got a lot of rotation... So the the Orion people out in L.A. saw that and liked the way she looked. She was also helpful in auditions for the actor that was going to play her boyfriend. Somewhere, in a carton in my basement, I have Madonna and Bruce Willis doing an early screen test for that."

Madonna's presence though, at a time when her fame was becoming stratospheric and every young girl wanted to look and dress like her, made this film the hit it was and gave it a much needed dose of natural charisma. Madonna's Susan is a magical creation, a careless and cool character who sort of strolls on to the screen and nonchalantly dominates any scene she is in. There's a naturalistic edge to it, and you get the impression she was getting a real buzz out of playing this free spirit, cruising from town to town looking for new adventures. She did her own hair and make up for the film too, so clearly she had a similar level of artistic control over her character as she did with her music.

Just how much of Madonna's role in the film is down to acting though is another matter. This is definitely a star performance and she is effortlessly magnetic whenever on the screen. Madonna is speaking her lines with coolness, as if she couldn't care less what anyone thinks and perhaps this is the key to why it was such an authentic characterisation. Maybe Madonna herself didn't care what anyone thought. She had bagged a part in a big movie, a now iconic role and clearly at the time, a much desired character. It was the perfect part for her - her first big appearance in the movies, in a role that combined her true self with a little touch of liberated movie exoticism. Madonna was just being naturalistic and cleverly altering already apparent facets of herself to fit in with Susan. Still, she holds her own with the more experienced Arquette and her other co stars, including a brilliant Aidan Quinn.

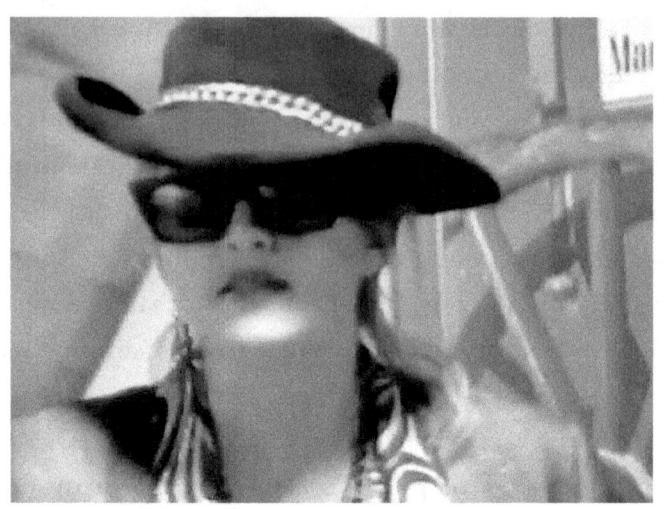

Madonna on set of Desperately Seeking Susan

Although her character is almost the whole of the 1980s personified into one pop cultural entity, there is also much more to it than that. Watching the plot becoming more daft and complex, you think back to classic cinema of yesteryear and those quirky female leads from the golden era; Audrey Hepburn at her kookiest, a touch of vintage Jane Fonda and Shirley MacLaine. It's the kind of star performance that is hard to define and a very old fashioned comedy in many ways; that glamorous presence, the few chosen words, the charm and the overwhelming appeal which makes every man in the film fall over themselves to get to her. It's remarkable that such an inexperienced actress could make such a big impression in her first film.

At the Los Angeles premier, fans gathered from miles around to catch a glimpse of their heroine arriving at the screening. In the video of the event, Madonna blows them all a kiss, playing the movie star with ease. She says of her character, "She's irresponsible, she's adventurous, she's courageous and she's very vulnerable." The interviewer asks, "Is she Madonna?" The Queen of Pop herself looks into the camera and tellingly replies "we have some things in common."

On the set of the movie itself, Madonna gave an interview for television, saying "I play Susan, a very free spirited femme fatale, charming everyone and breaking people's hearts. But everyone likes her because she represents fun and adventure." Again, she could have been talking about herself and she knew that very well.

Released the year I was born, this film has a lovely nostalgic feel to it now, with the music, the fashion and the dialogue. It's a perfect snapshot of a time, when Madonna's very appearance told you she was something unique. She has some wonderful moments throughout, not least her first appearance in the bedroom, snapping pictures of her one night stand and packing her suitcase up for the next chapter. Another great scene gives us a telling glimpse into how Susan lives her life, washing in a public rest room, oblivious to what the other women might think, as she dries her arm pits under the hand dryer. Yes Susan is wild, free and ready for the next thrill, but there is something almost childish behind this breezy, sharp dressed front. It's almost as if there's a hint of that little girl lost about her, somewhere deep inside perhaps.

Another stand out scene, perhaps the most famous in the movie, is when Madonna amusingly dances to her own song, the brilliant Into the Groove, in a smoky 1980s night club spot. Typically for Madonna, unarguably the greatest PR woman in the world, she makes sure we hear the song in its entirety, literally having to prick up our ears to pick out the dialogue from under the music. Now that's genius.

Madonna aside, the film flows wonderfully and the script is tight as can be. The supporting cast are all on top form too, working in aid of the farcical plot. It was a big hit at the time and proved successful with the critics too, who saw it as a charming throwback to the farces of the 1930s. I liken it to Woody Allen, in its tone, quirky characters, performance style and plot shifts.

Reviews at the time seem to agree it's a decent film, a somewhat freakish surprise hit that came from nowhere. Roger Ebert thought it was solid, commenting, "What I liked in Desperately Seeking Susan was the cheerful way it bopped around New York, introducing us to unforgettable characters, played by good actors. It has its moments, and many of them involve the different kinds of special appeal that Arquette and Madonna are able to generate. In a dizzying plot they somehow succeed in creating specific, interesting characters."

Retrospective reviews all seem to agree that it was the one definitive movie where Madonna found her perfect role. Time Out wrote that it was an "emancipated screwball comedy, even if the plotting is square as a square peg. Madonna has never found a better fit than the role of Susan, a thrift-store free spirit - and even then Arquette gives as good as she gets with a deliciously kooky comic turn."

Looking back on the classic movie, BluRay.com wrote "Desperately Seeking Susan has a fresh, youthful way about it that keeps it humming along when dramatics fail to earn interest. Perhaps this is the Madonna magic in motion, with the star's iconic style and

158

swagger sparking the picture to life whenever she's onscreen, creating a personal aura of irresistibility."

It has to be said that much of its success and longevity is down to Madonna's presence alone, even though the film still works on numerous levels. It caught her at that magic point in time, resulting in an explosive collision of star and movie that could never be repeated again.

The following year's film was not so praised though. The infamous flop that is Shanghai Surprise put massive bullet holes in the film careers of the-then husband and wife team of Sean Penn and Madonna, although they would both recover from its ice cold reception in time, one more so than the other. Close on to 30 years since its release, the movie is nowhere near as bad as people made out back in the day and to be honest, it's a pretty enjoyable little comedy in its own right.

Sean Penn plays Glendon Wasey, a con man selling glow in the dark ties in Shanghai. He comes across Gloria (Madonna), a nurse who is looking for a large quantity of opium for her sick patients. Wasey promises to help her get a hold of a shipment of opium coming in, but the fact that various unsavoury folk, such as gangsters and seedy lowlifes, are also after the loot adds many complications to the plot.

Produced and developed by George Harrison's Handmade Films company (although distributed by MGM), the film was an unexpected massive bomb, which is odd when you think of the collective profiles of its two stars. Penn and Madonna were at the centre of a whirlwind of press, their relationship pretty much being the focal point for the whole of the world media at that point in time.

Despite Madonna's recent success in the pop charts and the movie world with her previous picture, Shanghai Surprise suffered worse than anyone could have predicted. It's a curious thing really, as I always enjoyed the film, especially its broadly comic performances from Penn and the late, great Richard Griffiths. I also think Jim Goddard directs it very well and the whole thing has a hectic, fast pace that ensures it never drags. It's a charming film in my view, although it was so viciously panned that people never take you serious if you dare to like it.

Penn had already proved himself a decent comic performer by this stage, with his role in the 1982 comedy classic Fast Times At Ridgemont High. To prove he had true dramatic power, he was brilliant in At Close Range, released right before Shanghai Surprise (which itself boasted a classic Madonna single, Live to Tell). As Wasey, Penn is hilarious, embodying the required sleaze of this shady character, downing booze and shouting his mouth off boorishly. In contrast, Madonna plays the seemingly kind nurse very well, and those more familiar with Madonna's edgier screen presence may be surprised when watching her work here; that is of course if they reconsider this most misunderstood movie and give it another chance.

Still, you cannot argue with the figures. Costing 17 million dollars to make, it scraped back only 2 million at the US box office. Perhaps people were expecting so much from their dream celebrity couple that the results were only bound to disappoint. Plus, the reviews were as bad as can be, which obviously put them off going in the first place.

The New York Times were vicious, writing at the time "the nicest thing about Shanghai Surprise is that you can watch it in near-total privacy. At the first show at Loew's State, where the film opened Friday, there were barely enough bystanders to make up a baseball team."

The LA Times were unimpressed too, calling it "a movie of jaw-dropping, high-water mark dreadfulness. Give the film a Shanghai gesture and stay quietly home with a good book." While Time Out summed their review up with "the action is simply an implausible chain of events sensationally strung together, a Saturday morning serial formula which worked for Raiders of the Lost Ark; here, the heavy-handed manipulation of genre ingredients simply results in vulgar, often embarrassing, kitsch."

Madonna and producer George Harrison promoted the film heavily at the time and at the famous press conference held in London, Madonna answered questions for a hungry rabble of reporters. One journalist remarked that Madonna was a remarkable screen presence in Desperately Seeking Susan. "Thank you," Madonna smiled knowingly.

When asked about the plot of the movie, sitting beside a rather bored, gum chewing Harrison, Madonna saw something much closer to home than you'd think in her character. "It takes place in Shanghai, and I play a missionary... let's see," she said, pausing. "The reason I'm there is, well you have to think of the political climate in America, there was a depression and there weren't a lot of jobs; unemployment was at an all time high. There weren't a lot of opportunities for women, so rather than stay at home, get married and raise children or stand in a bread line or work in a sweat shop, I wanted to do something exciting with my life so I go to Shanghai to become a missionary and help people."

Harrison himself provided songs for the soundtrack and they actually fit some of the themes of the film pretty well. But for George, any efforts he put into the film proved to be all for not. Having made a series of lower budget, often stunning films, Handmade went big budget for Shanghai Surprise, the same year they made the terrific Mona Lisa starring Bob Hoskins. Putting the money up for this blockbuster comedy, Harrison perhaps felt a bit daft later on when the film didn't make any profit at all.

Interviewed for Creem Magazine about the film, Harrison had some not so kind words to say. "So it was disappointing because I think she (Madonna) was trying to be a little bit nice," Harrison said, "but she doesn't have a sense of humour, which is unfortunate. 'Cause it was a comedy."

Rather tellingly, he also expressed his view of why people thought the film didn't quite work, stating in 1987: "What went wrong with Shanghai Surprise? Well, we got the wrong script, the wrong director and the wrong stars. It was more of a case of, Where did I go right? It turned into a bloody nightmare. Let's just say that Madonna and Sean Penn could have been much better if they had not been hounded by the press and hounded by their own minds. It was the combination of her thinking she's a star and the way the press was gunning for her. The British press went after them like dogs chasing a bone. All this aloofness and star stuff… it's bullshit. I'm not trying to be nasty, she's probably got a lot in her that she hasn't even discovered yet, but she has to realise that you can be a fabulous person and be humble as well."

Despite its legendary status as a clunker, and it being nominated for Worst Film and Madonna "winning" Worst Actress at the Golden

Raspberry Awards, it really isn't all that bad. In fact I stand by my opinion that it's a decent little comedy and had it starred anyone else, the critics wouldn't have gone in with such premeditated views and I am sure it would have been a much better received picture. But it marked a beginning for Madonna's screen career where the press were ever ready with their daggers, to rip her acting work to shreds.

Unfortunately, especially given the hammering Shanghai Surprise had fallen victim to, Madonna's next movie also failed to match the box office success of Desperately Seeking Susan. By 1987, when Who's That Girl was released, Madonna was a bona fide pop megastar, and you could be forgiven in assuming that her legions of fans would have gone along to see any movie she was in. Unfortunately though, a lot of them didn't and as well as being a commercial flop, Who's That Girl also received just as many bad notices as Shanghai Surprise did.

The plot itself was good enough. Madonna played a framed ex convict being reluctantly escorted by stiff attorney Loudon Trott (Griffin Dunne), who is busy enough as it is with an impending wedding, and a rich father in law who entrusts him with various intimidating duties, including the transportation of a wild cougar. Madonna's Nikki Finn persuades Loudon to help her catch those pesky crooks who framed her and bring them to justice. In the meantime, Loudon falls for the wild girl who turns his life upside down.

It's funny when you discover something you always thought was really good turns out to be universally disliked by almost every source you look at. As a kid, Who's That Girl was played regularly in our house, both the music from it and the film itself. So it's odd to see how it supposedly failed on all accounts, if you read what the critics say that is. Again though, it doesn't change my opinion that it's a well made, often very funny slice of light 80s comedy.

Before Who's That Girl, director James Foley had worked with Madonna on some of her music videos. One of these was the classic Live to Tell, itself taken from Foley's movie At Close Range, starring none other than Sean Penn. Foley had even stood as best man at the pair's wedding, so Madonna definitely trusted him. Certainly no fool, Madonna wanted the talented director to head her next project, but she had to push hard in order to persuade Warner Brothers that she could deliver the goods, especially after the dismal failure of Shanghai Surprise. In truth, you can't really fault Madonna's efforts in the film. Looking like a punk rock Marilyn Monroe with bleached hair and red lipstick, we are in iconic Madonna territory here; the New York accent, incessant gum chewing and cocky attitude all combine to make one of her finest screen creations. She gets the chance to tackle some excellent scenes; one particularly cool moment arrives when Finn is being let out of prison after serving the four year sentence. "Am I free now?" she asks the guard. "Yeah you're free," they reply. As you would, Madonna gives them a smack around the chops, knocking them out cold on to their back. "Be nice" she calmly says before walking away. It's another wild, charismatic performance, the sort she could clearly excel at; an unhinged, yet finely tuned and controlled characterisation. She's not trying to consciously *be* anything other than this unpredictable woman, and it works on every level. For all her zest and lust for life, she makes Dunne's character realise that he's been living something of a boring existence until meeting her. This girl is the breath of fresh air he has been waiting for.

"I liked her dual personality," Madonna said of her character, obviously relating to Finn and seeing some of herself in her. "Her tough side and her sweet side. That's kind of what the movie's about. Sweetness and toughness. Obviously when there is a toughness it's only a mask for the vulnerability she feels."

Although it wasn't a massive hit anywhere, it did perform better abroad, but Madonna herself claimed that the film may have underperformed in the States because of her own massively scaled live show which was already under way, her first world wide venture in fact.

"I think the movie did badly in America because I upstaged it with my tour," she insisted. "People were confused about the connection between the record, the tour and the movie because they all had the same title. I also think there are people who don't want me to do well in both fields. I had to really fight to get any respect from the music business and now I guess there are some people who feel that I ought to be grateful for that respect and stick to music."

In her interview with Rolling Stone in 1987, she reflected on the lure of cinema, as well as the similarities between her music and the movies. She also addressed the difficulties some might have had with seeing her on the big screen. "Acting is fun for me," Madonna said, "because, well, for most people, music is a very personal statement, but I've always liked to have different characters that I project. I feel that I projected a very specific character for Like A Virgin and that whole business and then created a much different character for my third album. The problem is, in the public's mind, you are your image, your musical image, and I think that those characters are only extensions of me. There's a little bit of you in every character that you do. I think I had something in common with Susan in Desperately Seeking Susan, and I think I have a lot in common with Nikki Finn in Who's That Girl, but it's not me. Still, I wouldn't have been attracted to her if we didn't have something in common."

She makes a fair point. The public find it hard to digest too many public images and the critics didn't ever really *want* to like Madonna's movies and often seemed to delight in cutting her down. And they weren't going to pin the blame of Who's That Girl on a distracting world tour.

The Advocate spat: "Madonna delivers the worst performance in recent memory as the heroine of an attempt at screwball comedy. Watching her try to look like Marilyn Monroe and sound like Betty Boop, though, is a sure sign that this film was a disaster in the making. At the same time, it seems inconceivable that anyone would sit down and plan something so dreadful."

And yet The Washington Post's writer Hal Hinson admitted he found the film to be something of a guilty pleasure. "I admit to laughing at much of the movie," he wrote. "But go ahead, shoot me, I laughed. The animated title credits - which present Madonna as an amalgam of Betty Boop, Marilyn Monroe and Joan Blondell, strewing chaos in her wake - provide the key. The rest of the picture is just as cartoonish as the credits - only the characters are real."

The New York Times though seemed to genuinely enjoy Madonna's turn. "Whatever happened, two things are clear," they wrote. "Madonna, left to her own devices and her own canny pace, is a very engaging comedian, and the screenplay, by Andrew Smith and Ken Finkleman, contains a lot of raffishly funny ideas... When Madonna's no-nonsense pragmatism isn't being twisted into poses of lovable eccentricity, the actress is sexy and funny and never for a minute sentimental. At times she looks amazingly like Marilyn Monroe, but the personality is her own, more resilient and more knowing."

Still, Madonna insists the film is a miss, agreeing with many of the critics in this case. Asked by film critic Mark Greczmiel why both Who's That Girl and Shanghai Surprise hadn't performed well commercially, Madonna replied with sincere honesty. "Because they weren't very good movies," she said. "The script wasn't great. There are a million things that make a film work or not work, and what I learned from that is that I didn't think too clearly about those movies. It was like, I did Desperately Seeking Susan and someone handed me Shanghai Surprise and I was like, Oh yeah, I'll do that! I just wasn't paying a lot of attention to dialogue and structure. I was so eager to make movies."

Who's That Girl is a fun and charming comedy and Madonna is certainly funny in it. Take it on that level, as a breezy screwball comedy of its time, and I'm sure you'll enjoy the ride.

Madonna made one more movie before seeing out the 1980s. The first and final film directed by Howard Brookner, before his untimely death the following year, is a colourful comedy drama called Bloodhounds of Broadway, set in the late 1920s and based on four short tales written by Damon Runyon. It follows reporter Waldo Winchester getting deep into four separate potential news stories during a vibrant New Year's Eve celebration in 1928. One of the film's oddest little plots involves Randy Quaid playing Feet Samuels (named so for his oversized feet), a man hopelessly in love with showgirl Hortense Hathaway (Madonna). He is planning on having one last wild drunken night before committing suicide, because rather oddly, he has sold his body, or should I say his feet, to scientific research.

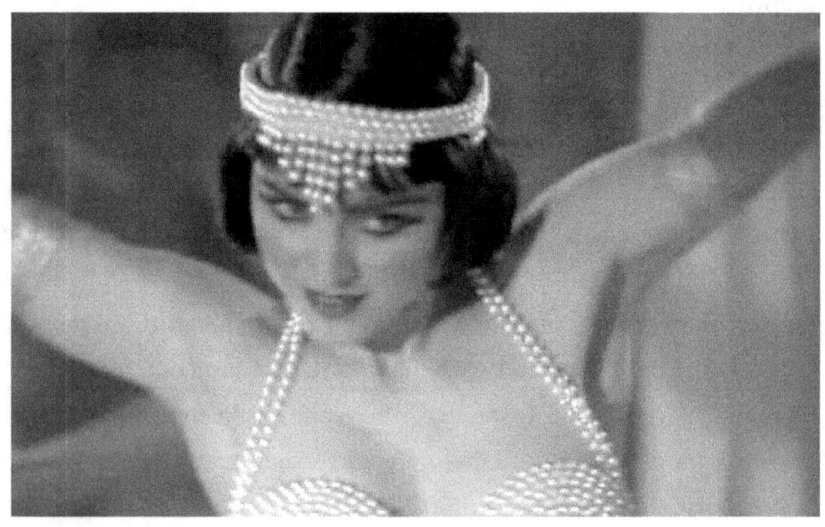

Bloodhounds of Broadway (1989)

Bloodhounds of Broadway was relatively low budget at 4 million dollars and despite its glittering all star cast (Matt Dillon, Jennifer Grey) it was still a flop, only making half a million back at the box office. But the film is engaging and there are some genuinely good moments in it. Madonna's on stage duet with Jennifer Grey, singing I

Surrender Dear, is a great scene, as the love struck Feet watches his object of desire in awe. Madonna handles the scene brilliantly, with the dazzling 1920s stage movements and side glances to Feet. It's similar in feel to one of her classic music videos from the era. It also stands as a precursor to Madonna's interest in the showbiz days of old, namely the 20s and 30s, and in particular to her role as chanteuse to the mob, Breathless Mahoney, in Dick Tracy the following year. She fit right into this era.

Howard had already been suffering from the AIDS that took his life when shooting commenced and clearly he was not a well man behind the camera. After filming was done, Howard called Madonna to tell her the news of his condition, but she admitted that she already knew. He asked her about a friend of hers who had been taken by the disease and in Madonna's words "wanted all the gory details" about the final days and how she had nursed him to the very end. In retrospect there is a bittersweet feel to the movie.

Again though, even though she was clearly good in the picture, her work went unappreciated in some quarters. Wrongly and predictably, she was nominated for yet another Razzie for Worst Supporting Actress. Watching her in the film though, I cannot see where they were coming from. By then I think it was the done thing for the Razzies; if Madonna happens to be in, slam it! Some critics couldn't get into the film itself though, as Vincent Canby of NY Times wrote "in spite of its large, talented cast, including Matt Dillon, Madonna, Julie Hagerty and Randy Quaid, Bloodhounds of Broadway never gets going. It ambles pleasantly. Even though the movie ends about 15 minutes before it actually stops, Bloodhounds of Broadway plays as if it were a series of vaguely connected opening sequences." While

Variety said the performances lifted the "fluffy" material, they even singled Madonna's performance out as "adept." Time Out too said the performances were good, "even Madonna's" they noted, before adding "Madonna's confession that she wants to drop being a jazz baby and retire to a 'quarter-acre in Newark' to raise babies and chickens might just be worth your attention."

Madonna would go on to do more movies in the next decade, some which did well (Dick Tracy, A League of Their Own, the towering Evita which won her a Golden Globe), and some which, well, didn't do well at all (Body of Evidence and Dangerous Game come to mind, two underrated gems in my view). By the end of 80s though, Madonna was the Queen of Pop who just happened to have had mixed dalliances with the film world. While filming her role in Beatty's Dick Tracy comic book epic, on set in 1989 on the cusp of a new decade, Madonna may have wondered where her movie career was heading...

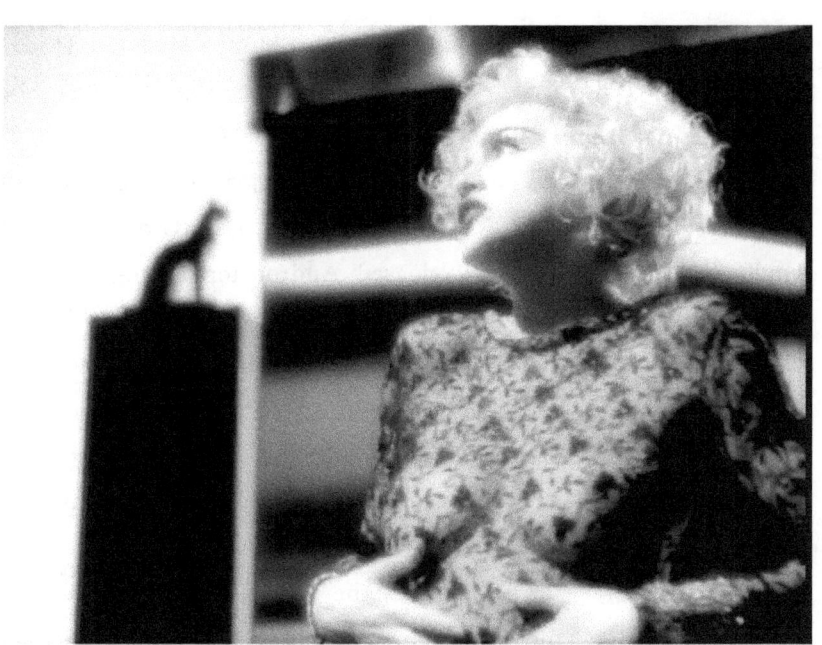

<u>1990</u>

HOW MADONNA KICKSTARTED
A NEW DECADE

Although some may argue that Michael Jackson was the maybe the main dominating force on the music industry and popular culture in the 1980s, there is also a case of Madonna being pretty much the sole figure who spent most time in the glare of the spotlight from 1983 right to the end of the decade. Though at the peak of his commercial powers, Jackson released only two albums in the whole ten years; yes, one of them was the most successful album of all time, Thriller, but it was hardly a prolific phase in his career. Madonna however, was ridiculously busy.

As well as recording four seminal studio albums - Madonna (1983), Like a Virgin (1984), True Blue (1986) and Like a Prayer (1989) - she also put out a remix album, You Can Dance (1988), released 26 singles, and starred in a handful of major movies, such as Desperately Seeking Susan (1985) and Who's That Girl? (1987), of which a soundtrack was also released. And on top of this were two high profile tours, The Virgin Tour and Who's That Girl? World Tour. Clearly, she never stopped. If people wondered why Madonna was never off the radio, off the TV or out of the newspapers, then it was because she worked so hard to consistently stay there. When she said she wanted to rule the world on her first major TV appearance on American Bandstand in 1984, she certainly meant it.

At the turn of the next decade, the 1990s, things changed for Madonna as they did for many people. While many of her contemporaries either slowed down, lost their way or drifted out of serious contention, Madonna went from strength to strength. She was still huge, in fact she became even more of a star, but the work she put out became much more challenging, controversial and to some, outrageous. When she had shocked in the 1980s, rolling around in orgasmic glee at major awards ceremonies and singing provocative lyrics, these "shock tactics" were nothing compared to what she would get up to in the 90s. Indeed, there had never been, and never will be again, a mainstream star exploring such avant-garde themes.

Back in 83 she was already desperate to shake off the disco tag she had gained on her first album. Fast forward a decade and she had recently recorded an erotic concept album (Erotica, released in 1992), where she adopted the character of Dita, starred in a steamy thriller (Body of Evidence) and stunned the world with her controversial, and

172

very daring, Sex Book. She was pushing further and further, taking her art closer to the boundaries than anyone else in the mainstream dared to.

If you consider the progress of her closest contemporary, Michael Jackson (on an influential and celebrity level at least), the juxtaposition was startling. Jackson had scored his mega hit with Thriller at the start of the 80s, and by the early 90s he had released 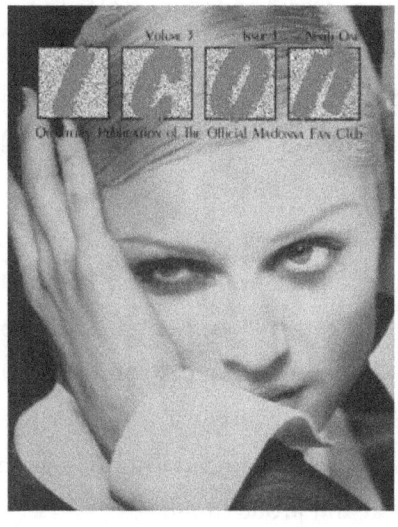 only two more albums (Bad and Dangerous), neither of which advanced his sound much. By the end of the decade, he had mutated into a cartoon of himself, a figure more known for his court cases, plastic surgery and rabid spending than his music. Madonna, while becoming a very polarising figure in the 1990s, was undoubtedly still challenging herself, and of course her audience too. For that she must be admired.

Few musical artists release one of their most iconic moments nearly a decade into their public career, but Madonna did just that in March of 1990, when she unleashed on the world her latest single, the remarkable, catchy-as-hell Vogue. The first single from her first album of the 90s, I'm Breathless (the soundtrack spin off to her latest hit movie, Dick Tracy), Vogue was Madonna at her catchiest, most vital, and it has to be said, most shamefully camp. Much imitated and loved for close to thirty years, it's quintessential Madonna, so engraved into the public consciousness and parodied that it's easy to overlook its genius. It really is a slice of pop perfection, with a wonderful video to boot, which features Madonna at her most striking and appealing.

If you look at 1990 as a whole, it's a staggering year for Madonna's career. In many ways, 90 was the year of Madonna, for it featured a hit album in I'm Breathless, a successful, acclaimed performance as sexy Breathless Mahoney in Dick Tracy, world wide hit singles in the form of Vogue, Keep It Together, Justify My Love and Hanky Panky, one of the best selling greatest hits packages in Immaculate Collection, and one of the most lucrative and legendary tours of all time with her brilliant Blond Ambition Tour. Phew...

It's kind of fitting that the new decade, the new artistic dawn, should start with such a strong statement. Sure, it wasn't her first single of the 1990s (that goes over to Keep It Together, culled from the Like A Prayer album, released in 1989), but it was the first real moment the world realised that Madonna wasn't just a fad for the 1980s. As if she hadn't proved herself enough with that run of classic albums and singles, here she was, loud and proud in the 90s.

With those opening keyboard strings bringing us into Madonna's declaration that everyone can dance and feel good (feel like a star in fact) if they just strike a pose, the claps and hi hat get the mood going. Then it's that danceable beat, and the subtle musical flourishes, which ensure the song instantly get its hooks into you. Madonna's voice, clearly recorded and produced by co-writer Shep Pettibone, is at its most effortlessly iconic, the singing is precise, while the spoken word finale is sexy and intimate.

"Everyone has their sexuality. It's how you treat people in everyday life that counts, not what turns you on in your fantasy."

- Madonna

It seems that every female pop star these days uses sex as a tool to sell herself, her brand and her product to the wider public. Now, in the present day, sex is just a part of the whole package, as accepted as the song and the music video as a selling device. But this wasn't the case back in the 1980s. When Madonna flirted with these themes on the likes of Like A Virgin, many were shocked to say the least. But this was over thirty years ago, long before she drew a line in the sand and, for want of a better word, redefined what one woman could do in pop, and what was no longer off limits.

The first time she really shocked the masses by "using" sex was in 1990. Madonna had been scantily clad in various pop videos before Justify My Love, but something about that strange song and its even stranger video created a frenzy of outrage among critics and the more liberal of the general public. We were used to slightly risqué videos by then, skimpy outfits and innuendo, but Justify My Love was something else entirely. A sexy video in a time when sexy videos didn't exist, it featured a somewhat hazy Madonna in a night gown over her bra, knickers and suspenders, making her way to a kinky party in a hotel room, where she takes part in erotic experimentation with men and women. Nowadays, it's probably quite tame in its nudity and explicitness compared to modern pop video standards, but its artiness, black and white cinematography, moody performances and steamy goings on make it a very effective piece of forbidden sensuality, like a glance into the sexual fantasies of many a man and

175

woman who wouldn't own up to such dreams. The song is Madonna at her breathy best, and although a co-write, it's one of her classics.

Still, you can't get past the fact that the video is actually subtle when looking back on it, and it's hard to see why such a fuss was caused, and why indeed MTV banned the thing. People Magazine recently wrote "Given all the controversy about Madonna using the video to promote sex, sadomasochism, cross-dressing and whatever else critics perceived in it, it just doesn't seem quite so racy 25 years later. It's all about sex, sure, and it's very sexy, but the most scandalous thing in it is a woman who's topless except for a pair of suspenders that (mostly) cover her nipples. Of course, the female nipple is still a controversial body part today, but give the video a spin now and decide for yourself if you should be offended."

For Madonna though, the song and video was also a challenge. "When I did my Vogue video," she said in one TV interview, "there's a shot of me where I'm wearing a see-through dress, and you can clearly see my breasts. They told me that they wanted me to take that out, but I said I wouldn't, and they played it anyway. I thought that I was once again going to be able to bend the rules a little bit. I would like to address the whole issue of censorship on television. Where do we draw the line in general? I draw the line in terms of what I think is viewable on television. I draw the line at violence and humiliation and degradation."

So even if Madonna was being purposely controversial, she was at least doing it for a reason. Her "descent" into society's hidden, secret sexual underbelly was for a reason, to point out that sex itself is not a sin and as long as it's safe and consenting, no one is being hurt. You see things a hundred times more shocking and gratuitous on the news, so why get so wound up about a bit of semi-nudity? Madonna had a point, and her knack of winding up the stiff mainstream establishment of the early 1990s not only drew attention to the ludicrous nature of the bans and sense of hysterical outrage, but it also paved the way for future artists to freely explore their sexuality in their art.

The 1980s had been monumentally inspired and influential, but Madonna's story was in many ways just getting started. And so, the 1990s were born...

References and Acknowledgements

Thanks to Ed Steinberg, Jerome Sirlin, Dean Gant, Bruce Gaitsch, Leora Barish and George Du Bose for their recollections

The following sources were helpful;

Magazines and websites;
New York Times
LA Times
Variety
Rolling Stone
The Face
Island
Smash Hits
NME

Books:
Like An Icon, Lucy O'Brien
Madonna Megastar
Madonna Style, Carol Clerk
Madonna, by Marie Cahill
The Style Book, Debbi Voller
Madonna, Andrew Morton
Madonna On Screen, Chris Wade
The Music of Madonna, Chris Wade
Her Story, Michael McKenzie
Madonna by David James

Any Madonna fan knows about the many great website out there dedicated to her life and work; I want to thank Madonna Underground (they always support my Madonna books) and All About Madonna, an amazing resource on the Queen of Pop.

The images in this book are either public domain pictures or screenshots from live footage and promo videos, used via fair use in conjunction with criticism and commentary on the said films and music videos.

ABOUT CHRIS WADE

Chris Wade runs the acclaimed recording project Dodson and Fogg, on which the likes of Scarlet Rivera and Hawkwind's Nik Turner have appeared. He's written books on The Kinks, Madonna, Bob Dylan, Orson Welles, Robert De Niro and many others, and has also released audiobooks of his comedic fiction, narrated by such actors as Rik Mayall. His other work includes Rainsmoke, a recording project with actor Nigel Planer and the ongoing Hound Dawg Magazine. His first film, The Apple Picker, was released in 2017.

More info at his website: wisdomtwinsbooks.weebly.com

Email the lad: wisdomtwinsbooks@hotmail.com